Lump

-

David Moynihan

GW00480779

Table of Contents

Esther and Martin

"There are not enough words
to express a man's gratitude,
for saving a young boy's life.
Till the day we meet again".

-David

About the Author

From Notting Hill to Shepherds Bush, his journey began in the early 1960s. Born of an Irish immigrant family, David grew up on one of the toughest council estates in London. An-all-too familiar story with a lot of boys from these environments, he dreamt of being a footballer. But even before he left primary school, he discovered another world. *Gambling!*

It was this calling, that led him on a path of adventure from London to Miami, the Bahamas, New York, Los Angeles and many more exotic locations, too numerous to mention.

A natural born numbers-man, follow David's career as he finds himself in all sorts of hilarious situations including a scenario with his grandmother, the local priest and their parrot (Maggie), to a deal that went horribly wrong in Bermuda.

An extraordinary set of circumstances gave him the opportunity to take part in various nefarious activities including importing copious amounts of cocaine from the Bahamas into Miami, to dealing an illegal craps game for the mob in the Upper East side of Manhattan. But after twenty years, David called it a day, as by now, he was a father with two small children (Liam & Kate).

What followed was a ten-year stint in the poker world, first as a player, then as a dealer, before eventually becoming a Tournament Director on some of the biggest tours in Europe.

These days David can be found in Brighton, England, working as a Security Operative (bouncer), where the journey it seems, never ends.

Hope you enjoy the book.

David

Part 1

1

From all four corners of The Emerald Isle, they came-a-sailing in their hordes. The source of their invasion was a greyhound. Strong of limb and fleet of foot, it carried the hopes of an entire nation. The dog racing fraternity were hoping to witness one of the quickest dogs in history, race to victory in the fastest time ever recorded. A race over five hundred metres to determine who holds sway in the English/Irish greyhound world.

The energy created by the Celtic tiger was so palpable, you could feel it, smell it, you could fucking touch it. The weight of expectation was in the air. The sheer force of nature that was *Indian Joe* was about to be released onto the 'field of dreams' of West London.

On a typically balmy summer evening, a throbbing mass of some sixty thousand expectant fans descended on Shepherds Bush to watch the final of the Greyhound Derby.

In the lead up to the big day, I was given the heads-up by my grandfather Martin Power. Originally from Waterford in Ireland, he had friends in the business. Tall, dashingly handsome, grey haired at twenty-two with piercing blue eyes, he was a man of the community, all eighteen stones of him. Captain of the pub darts team, builder, surveyor, good card player, wheeler-dealer, a typical lump of an Irishman no one fucked about with. Early doors he knew I was mad about the dogs, so I will never forget those magical words,

"Listen here son, I've got a little tip. There's a dog coming over that's gonna win the Derby". End of conversation.

Although my grandparents claimed they were oblivious to the fact I used to go to the dogs, they knew it was a ritual of mine. I used to bunk off school on a Monday specifically to analyse the trials. I saw it as research, as I was gaining valuable information and insight into what trainers expected from a dog. How quick were they out of the traps? Did they prefer the inside or outside? What was the best trap to start? Crucial information a trainer would need to know. So, armed with the inside track from Grandad, I went in search of what was fast becoming the worst kept secret in the dog racing world.

As I approached the stadium preceding the Derby heats, there was something immediately obvious. What would usually be akin to a ghost town was no more. On any other Monday double figures were the norm, but on this occasion, there was an air of expectancy so compelling that it drew a sizeable crowd. I could see him from the other side of the stadium as he was led to the traps. I had seen this picture a thousand times, but there was something regal about him. Bred to within an inch of his life, he was as beautiful a greyhound the world had ever seen. Sinewy and strong, lithe and powerful, if there is a god in the dog world, then this was his son.

I started to get butterflies as the hare hit the line and the dogs were released. I will never forget the feeling that still resonates with me today. To see something of such beauty so in tune with what it was put on this earth to do was breath-taking. Everyone around was of the same mindset. As he flew out of the traps into his stride and down the back straight, we all just stared in amazement at the speed and grace that was *Indian Joe*. After he had finished destroying the White City track, we all scurried off, contemplating what we had just seen. I ran home to tell Grandad the good news. There was so much excitement coursing through my veins that I could barely get my words out. When he managed to get a word in, he stated in a thick Irish brogue, "Sure, I told you that"!

Needless to say, Grandad was delighted, and he was even happier when I told him he flew through his heats with ease. The quarters and semis came and went before we finally arrived at the day of reckoning. *He* was placed in Trap 6, his favourite. From a strategic standpoint, this was good news as had he been placed in Trap 5, it could have been problematic as the joint favourite, who was also an outside runner, was as quick to the bend and may cause traffic problems. However, once the draw had been made, we were a little relieved and now looked forward to the contest with relish.

The day was flying-by, so I went in search of some new clobber. On my way to Stuart's menswear on the Uxbridge Road W12, a now-famous clothing emporium that served up the rude boys from White City and beyond, I became acutely aware of something unusual. The whole environment felt out-of-place. It was a warm sunny Saturday, but I had never been in the presence of this many people in *The Bush* before. Every spiv, shyster, gangster, bookie and trader, was there. In all their glory, they were on display for this occasion. Young and old, chic and decidedly unfashionable, this was the time of the football fashion explosion, and Stuart's was at the root of that era.

For all English racing fans, the country look of Barbour, flat caps, brogues and relevant accessories were the order of the day. Among our Irish brothers however, it was suits with a collar and horrendous kipper tie. Given the fact there were at least thirty to forty thousand of them in attendance, the fashion police would have had a field day.

I was browsing, but I couldn't focus properly as my mind was all over the place. The nerves were starting to get the better of me too, so I went next door into The White Horse for a couple of beers to take the edge off.

After I had sorted me self out, I made my way to the Arena for the first race. White City Stadium was majestic. Built to house the 1908 Olympics, it stood the test of time. Now owned by the GRA, it was the home of greyhound racing in the UK!

I had drunk three bottles of beer and in the process of ordering my fourth when it dawned on me, I didn't feel anything. Such was my focus and concentration I had no buzz from the alcohol. I didn't even notice the crowd, with untold thousands outside. This had to stop because I wasn't enjoying myself. I wasn't doing anything. In terms of a profession, you could say this was my job. Even though I worked full-time, this was much more exciting, and I made more money out of it.

The minimum bet on a forecast was ten pence. For example, you bet ten pence that Trap 6 will win and Trap 1 will come second. If that is the outcome you win, if it isn't, you don't. It's as simple as that. This was causing me a little anxiety as the big event was fast approaching. One more race and then it's time.

This is what we've been waiting for. One month's work condensed into the next thirty seconds. He was odds-on joint favourite, so the track-side bookies would not take a pound note on him winning. They would only accept a bet on who came second however, you could place him in a forecast with the track. The second favourite Trap 5 also ran wide, the difference with him was, he cut in at the bend very sharp. Traps 1 and 2 were also well fancied. The issue with Trap 1 was his size and Trap 2 only came good in the second half. Meaning, if Indian Joe got a good start and stayed out of trouble at the first bend then (Trap 5) could only come second at best. I bet 5, would baulk the much smaller 1 dog at the first and the 2 dog, would follow Indian Joe home. Armed with fifteen pounds, I placed a wager on that prediction.

The introduction of the dogs was sounded by a trumpet. One by one they were led out, with the biggest cheer of the evening reserved for Trap 6. Louder and louder, the volume was increasing as punters attempted to place a bet. My mouth was dry, a little sweat began on my brow and my heart started to pump a little harder.

The lights around the stadium were switched off, so the dogs would have no distractions. As the hare made its way around the track, the crescendo of noise as the traps opened was off-the-scale.

What say you Indian Joe?

In the blink of an eye, he gave us the answer we had all come to see. The explosion of grace and power as he hit the front from the off was a once-in-a-lifetime event. About a hundred yards from the finish line, I saw it unfold. As I predicted, 5 cut in and baulked 1. It was a nasty collision that ended their night, and like a biblical passage to the Promised Land, Trap 2 rose like a phoenix out of the carnage. My heart was pumping like a jackhammer as the analysis I foresaw was about to be proven true. He missed the record by a couple of hundredths of a second, but I didn't care as 2 maintained his form, following the king of king's home and finishing second. The roar of the crowd as he crossed the line was colossal, what a race, what a dog. A true champion of champions. A minute after the finish an official announced in a voice that echoed throughout the stadium.

4

'*Winner Trap 6, second Trap 2*'. The forecast paid three pounds forty-seven pence for a ten pence stake, and I had it one hundred and fifty times, five hundred and twenty smackers if you please. You cannot imagine how satisfied I felt. It was the prediction of how the race would unfold that was the most satisfying. I had never felt such a feeling of accomplishment. As I collected the winnings, a curious thing happened, the cashier looked at me and said, '*ere mate, do you know Pecky?*'

The next day was a bit of a blur as we celebrated the win. Five hundred pounds in 1980, was a lot of money so Grandad and I had a few in The Smuts, an archetypal estate pub that only people who come from an estate would know. A real den of iniquity where outsiders would have been made to feel most unwelcome. The beer flowed, we laughed, it was a great day. The Smuts shut at 2:30 pm on a Sunday in those days which was a good thing as Nan had prepared one of her special roasts. After eating everybody had a snooze but I was on fire. It was a time for critical thinking, a time for reflection. What did I want to do with my life? What was I good at? What did I enjoy doing? More importantly, who the fuck is Pecky?

In amongst the great day that was yesterday, the boys that I found spellbinding were the trackside bookies, the settlers. Sharply dressed, with mouths to match, they took bets in seconds and on last night's action they took hundreds on any race at any given time. Sharp as a nail and bang on point, I was captivated.

My introduction into the gambling game had started early, I was taught how to play patience or solitaire as it is more commonly known by Grandad. He didn't make a point of giving me instruction, I watched him and learned how to play. I found a deck of cards fascinating. I taught myself the odds of probability as my belief even then was that cards were not a science-based on conjecture but a game of skill. I was considered a good three-card-brag player and I had dealt a seven-card-stud poker game. Throw in the fact I felt I was as quick as them in taking and paying out bets, I decided I wanted to be a dealer. I knew the odds of probability, I understood odds both fractional and decimal, it seemed a natural fit. But that's not how it started, it was a council estate game played by council estate kids both in the manor and at school where it all began. It could get violent at times, but it was intoxicating. It was after playing this I knew I was destined for a career in the gambling field.

2

Only when schools out do you realise, they are the best days of your life. Not only as an exercise in education but in finding where you fit in, what you are capable of. I was an average child from an average immigrant family. I went to Bentworth Primary School in White City, a breeding ground for scallywag's, rascals and Herbert's.

This was a time that even though we shared a classroom, the girls and we had separate playgrounds. As a young man I was painfully shy, and I am certain being separated at playtime only made it worst. The kids of today are a lot more forward as they have access to social media and the thousands of introductory platforms that entails. Call it evolution if you like, but I think it is about the mobile world today. They would have found it strange as we didn't require a regular dopamine hit. Another bizarre issue is the obesity problem. In previous years, exercise was the order of the day. After school, we played football, rugby, cricket, rounders, British Bulldog and many others too numerous to mention. In today's digital world it is all about staring at screens, is it any wonder that we have a problem with people's fatness? I remember how games of football were played with twenty-five on each side. There wasn't a single fat kid in sight. It was constant exercise and as we had little money, there were no take-aways. It baffles me that scientists and God knows who else derive all these theories about our weight problem when the answer to obesity is so very simple. Eat less, exercise more!

Around the age of seven your personality begins to form. The traits and idiosyncrasies that are a part of your make-up have already been shaped. The friendships you create in the classroom and at home with your parents and siblings are ingrained in your brain. You know how to manipulate your guardians, which buttons to press when you want something, and you are aware of when not to misbehave.

Life on a Council Estate was fantastic. It was around the age of eight that I discovered my calling. I was coming home from school when I noticed a group of boys playing a game I hadn't

7

seen before. They were getting excited and agitated at the same time. When it was one of the boy's turns to have a go, it went deathly silent, but once there was a result the threat of violence was never far away. It was intoxicating. My nerves were tingling, my pulse started to beat a little faster, I inched closer to get a better look then I asked the question. "What's this called"?

"Penny-up-the-wall!"

"D'you wanna play?"

It was quite intimidating, but I carried on watching regardless as I found the atmosphere enthralling. I had no concept of money as you take no part in the economic cycle. It is your grand/parents that stress about readies. All we did was eat, play, go to school, and sleep. However, this got me thinking. Why did I have these feelings as I only ever got excited about football?

In one foul swoop, my focus changed. I had an epiphany that developed into a paradigm shift in my long-term strategy. I was good at football, but I knew I was not going to make it as a pro. Even at that age, there are little pockets of info you retain which cause your juices to flow, and I knew in this game I had found something more interesting. Don't get me wrong I love football today as much as I did then, but I don't or never have got the same emotion out of the research and analysis of getting a bet right. Some call it a bet, some call it a gamble, in the stock market it is called a trade under the guise of a financial instrument, but whichever way you dress it up, it is all under the same umbrella.

Gambling!

Having discovered a potential new vocation in life, I set about obtaining the funds to take part. I had to come up with something quick as this new phenomenon was gaining momentum. Crowds were getting bigger meaning the prize pools were growing. Kids on every corner were playing it. My mind was in overdrive thinking of ways to get the readies and then it came to me in a flash of inspiration. The ice-cream man. On a personal note, I am a Motown, Elvis, Luther Vandross kind of guy but those dulcet tones that would explode from his van were a joy to behold. A ninety-nine with double flake, hundreds and thousands with chocolate sauce, a heart attack in a cone. I devised a cunning plan. Every day during the summer, the van would visit our estate at least once, so even though we were on a tight budget, they would furnish me with a shilling to buy ice cream. However, I would use the readies in my gambling studies. One shilling consisted of five pennies, which meant I had at least five goes at winning the prize.

Penny-up-the-wall looks easy but as anyone successful will tell you, winning entails graft. It takes research, development, guile, and no little skill. In most cases, it takes years of hard work depending on whatever your chosen field. Therefore, being so young left me at the mercy of much older boys.

The rules of the game are simple. You stand a certain distance from a wall and throw a penny at it. Whoever is closest to the wall wins. Sounds easy right? Try telling that to a darts player trying to hit a bull's eye to win a competition, a cricketer bowling someone out with the last ball of an innings, or a footballer taking the last penalty in a shoot-out. It looks easy, but it is nerve-shattering. There are many anomalies and inconsistencies that come into play that influence the outcome. Don't get me wrong, I am not suggesting that by winning a game of penny-up-the-wall can you be described as an Olympic champion, but it takes an element of skill to be consistently good at it.

If you were new to the game, the fanny they used to extract your investment became more outrageous as the game grew in popularity. Things like, 'he's from the block across the road', meaning they had the right to the money. It worked in most cases, but I was having none-of-it! I got a slap on the odd occasion, but I had learned the art of negotiation by this point. I was starting to spring up too, meaning the bullies left me alone. Even though you may hear an adult say something like, "He's only a baby, he wouldn't do things like that". Don't fucking kid yourself.

Over the course of the next couple of weeks I became quite good. I managed to claw back what I lost over the previous weeks. However, the end of the summer meant no more ice-cream man, meaning no more coinage and as penny-up-the-wall was an all-seasons game, this was a potential problem. My life in the 'world of readies' had begun, and I was not about to let it go so I came up with a plan. I would get a job. Grandad had been a milkman when he came over initially and as such, he had a relationship with our milkman who was looking for a little helper on a Saturday morning. A simple task of fetching and carrying bottles to and from doors on the estate. It was a good little number.

I was starting to develop a fondness for the game inside because we could keep everyone entertained in a warm environment, which was handy because it gave me the opportunity to develop my public relations skills.

In the sixties and seventies, the emphasis on entertainment was very much based around music as we only had two or three TV channels. We had a thing where couples slow danced together called the erection section, which left you in no doubt as to your dance partners intentions. This was key in keeping people entertained, yet another factor in why there were no fat kids in sight.

Modern technology was a long way from invention, so there were no mobiles, tablets, laptops etc. Cyberspace or the digital world has given us a more sophisticated opportunity to gamble, but in my day, it was all about using the tools at your disposal and in penny-up-the-walls case, you couldn't get a more primitive form of gambling. An essential ingredient in my tutorial was watching your pals' personalities develop. Sleight of hand, smoke and mirrors, even cheating, were used to win your money. However, in my case, I used these games to watch what was going on. Not just the technique it took to win but the players themselves. Any poker professional will tell you, it's not just about the hand and its possibilities, but the player and their previous strategy too.

I found it fascinating from the off. I was only a child, but I knew this was where I belonged. Penny-up-the-wall and soon to be learnt patience or solitaire were going to give me a skill set that's with me today. My mind developed the art of working out variables. I was four years away from going to the dogs, but I already knew I was comfortable in this environment.

Penny-up-the-wall launched my career into a life of travelling the world and working in places that I never thought possible.

I learned the skill to debate, the art of dodge and weave, and most importantly, the gift of *having it on me toes*, when I knew it was on top.

3

White City Estate, Shepherd's Bush, London W12, was built in the late 1930's to house the growing population of the working class. An estate of enormous proportions is bordered on the South by Loftus Road, the home of Queens Park Rangers, on the east by White City Stadium, home of the 1908 Olympics, on the west by Bloemfontein open-air swimming baths, Christopher Wren comprehensive, and the flower estate, and on the north by Hammersmith Hospital, Clement Danes grammar, Wormwood Scrubs prison and the Scrubs playing fields, home to many a Sunday morning scrap, otherwise known as a game of football.

A densely populated part of West London that prided itself on the number of villains and footballers it produced. Not only steeped in history, but because of its large Irish and Caribbean influence, one of culture, music and fashion.

Growing up in The City was tough, but enjoyable. My sister and I spent the first five years of our lives in Notting Hill with parents that divorced after what can only be described as a somewhat acrimonious union. So, we were now under the custodianship of our grandparents; It was a melting pot and eclectic mix of English, Irish and Caribbean working-class families that led very traditional lives. Dad went to work whilst Mum looked after the saucepan lids. A proverbial city within a city.

We lived in a three-bedroom flat in Bathurst House, we only had to lift the dogs up and they were off, the cat came and went with impunity, and the parrot terrified the life out of anyone that came near our balcony. As well as housing a goldfish and a hamster, we had our own little zoo going on.

Football games could get lairy, for example, our motto was one of go out for a fight, and if someone wants to throw a ball in, we'll have a game of football as well. But the overriding aspect in all of this was we had fun, particularly where house parties were concerned because our Caribbean brothers and sisters brought us their food and, more importantly reggae music.

11

To this day, oxtail and dumplings is still one of my favourite meals alongside listening to the Mighty Diamonds.

Anyway, I was twelve now, and by virtue of my mother, life was about to take a very welcome twist. She used to run a little kiosk at the stadium selling confectionary and needed help for a big Speedway event.

As I approached the stadium, I got butterflies. I understood and felt its history. I got knots in my stomach, the scale, noise, the crowd was a bit of me.

I found myself in a moment of gladiatorial proportions. I thought about the champions that had been and gone and the champions to come. What went on here? Where did all these people come from? The innumerable questions were rolling around in my head, so imagine my surprise when I learned it was used primarily for greyhound racing.

I was familiar with dog racing as I used to go coursing in Clonmel, Ireland, but it was held in a field where a hare was let free, and the dogs went in pursuit. 'Where do the dogs run?

The dogs are placed in traps 1-6, and then an electric hare is released. The traps open, with the first across the line the winner.

On the following Tuesday, I noticed two older boys bunking in. I approached at speed catching them off-guard, and before they could say anything, I was in. Even at such a young age, I could get away with being eighteen, I was already close to six feet tall, so I could walk around the stadium unchallenged, as there was no such thing as ID. If you looked old enough, you were in. What immediately struck me was the professionalism of everyone. Research and analysis were at the core of business here as it was about the dogs, their preparation, the last four races, what class they ran at, what trap they ran from, did they hit the first bend hard, were they wide runners, their weight, did they favour the conditions? All these permutations to consider and more.

As the trumpets sounded for the introduction of the dogs, you notice an immediate jump in volume as excitement builds. The trackside bookies sound their odds. The bell sounds, the lights go dim as they release the hare. The dogs fly out of the traps to a crescendo of noise, the race finishes, the lights get turned back on, and the whole process starts again.

I must have stood there motionless for about five minutes, when one of the boy's approached me. "Were you on? Did you back it?" I was completely unfamiliar with betting terminology, so I said no!

When I got in Nan was not amused!

"Where the fuck have you been"?

"I lost track of time".

"Lying toe-rag".

She saw straight through it and grounded me for two weeks. After the time had lapsed, I overheard two older boys at school talking about the greyhound stadium needing pot men.

"What's a pot man"?

"You pick up empty glasses and clean ashtrays"!

Basically, you went around picking up empty bottles and glasses, and helped restock the shelves when they needed replenishing.

"How do I apply"?

"You don't Dumbo. Just go to the stadium".

And so it came to pass, I got the job and started on the following Saturday.

4. Esther Power nee; (Wall)

They gained the nickname '*the black Walls*' by virtue of their skin. Nan didn't need a two-week stint on the Costa Brava, she would have got the same colour on a lunchbreak. Born and bred in Carrick-On-Suir, Tipperary, Eire. Four-foot-nothing with jet black hair and olive skin, she was the youngest of eight born to Patrick and Biddy Wall. A dressmaker by trade, butter wouldn't melt in her mouth kind of gal, but good luck if you got on the wrong side of her. Sharp as nails and tough as old boots. When she lost her temper, I used to bolt over the balcony and let Grandad kop for it. I'd be at the window, laughing my bollocks off as she unleashed the dogs of hell on him. He would have felt the full force of the two dogs Biscuit and Hector, Sylvia the cat, Maggie the parrot, Harry the hamster, even the fucking goldfish would have gone steaming in

Nan and Grandad emigrated here on St. Patrick's Day in forty-eight with their daughter Alice, carrying the dream of finding work as at home, prospects were somewhat dire. Arriving in Paddington, they were told the streets of London were paved with gold however, this could not have been further from the truth. Whilst in the search for accommodation in Notting Hill, a common denominator in big, bold letters was printed on doors,

'*No Irish, no blacks, no dogs need apply!*'

However, with a bit of luck, they managed to find accommodation in Paddington whilst they set about finding employment. Grandad found work as a milkman, and Nan a job in the sweatshops of the East End making clothes, all-in-all a good result.

Then one day, a colleague asked if she wanted a little cleaning job in Holland Park as she was finding it difficult to combine two jobs. Money was tight, so Nan accepted the opportunity of a trial.

On that morning, the prince came out of his room bemoaning the fact that his shirt had a defect, so she offered to fix it for him. Said shirt mended and freshly ironed gave Nan some momentum. She made Rupert breakfast, and after careful consideration with his wife Josephine, she was offered a permanent position on the spot. From modern-day-slavery in an east-end, sweatshop to working for the aristocracy in one fail swoop.

Fiercely protective of that family and secretive until the day she died, no one would have known what she did.

Rupert Lowenstein, a merchant banker by trade, was credited with the financial success of the Rolling Stones, and as such, Nan developed personal relationships with them too. Very occasionally, she would recite old anecdotes about The Stones including the time that Keith Richards turned up having bought three new shirts that were deliberately fashionably crinkled. On seeing said shirts, Nan proceeded to iron them, leaving Mr. Richards somewhat perplexed.

"Nan, any danger you could mend my trousers for me as I've got an ole in 'em?

"You've got another one up your arse, do you want me to sew that up for you too"?

Me and the boys were going to Bournemouth for a night out, so we got some 'black-bombers' for the trip. If you are not familiar with these pills, they were prescribed for people with obesity to quell their hunger, with the side-effect that you could drink like a fish, not get drunk and stay awake for days. We did Bournemouth Fri/Sat/Sun, got back about 10pm and decided the Burlington in Chiswick was our last port of call. We had a couple more as a night-cap, were in the process of walking out, when a pal of ours buys me and Timmy a drink. Considering he and I had been up for nearly four days; we had the additional beer and went to KFC on the way home.

With a bucket of chicken, we arrive at the flat, when we realized our *friend* had spiked our drinks! We were twitching for England, and not in the slightest bit hungry. I hadn't noticed Tim's absence, so it came as some surprise when he re-appeared, stark bollock naked apart from a scarf around his neck and proceeded to jump all over the front room furniture. After about five minutes he ran out of steam, so he's sitting opposite us with his eyes popping out of his head, panting like a maniac, gurning like fuck with his Hampton dangling between his legs. Nan said,

'David, will you tell Timmy to straighten up the cushions'

She was a God-fearing woman but was averse to going to church herself, so my sister and I had to go to Sunday school as she was fiercely proud of being Catholic.

I was roughly twelve at the time, and Grandad was assisting the local priest in renovating the estate youth club which had gone into a state of disrepair then arranged to come around for lunch to have a meeting. The problem, however, were the animals, particularly our parrot Maggie who had a penchant for using expletives when Grandad was about.

Fifteen minutes before the priest arrived, Nan asked me to move Maggie into my room and place a blanket over his cage so that he thought it was night-time and go to sleep. Nan then parked herself in the front room whilst I very conveniently forgot to remove the parrot. The doorbell goes, so I run excitedly to answer as I know the full extent of what is about to happen.

I answer the door to be greeted by the priest who introduces himself, and I walk him slowly down the hallway and into the *theatre of dreams*. Nan stands up and greets the priest with a heartfelt 'hello, father', which is very quickly met with a burst of wolf whistles and an indescribable, beautiful, almost soulful bellowing of 'hello, hello' from Maggie. Then Grandad walks in, and in somewhat dulcet tones, says, "hello, father" swiftly followed by the parrot,

"Bollocks, fuck off to bingo, you fucking fat cunt".

Cue pandemonium. Biscuit started attacking Hector, who was desperately trying to shag her because she was on heat. The goldfish was swimming at a hundred miles an hour because the cat had her paw in the bowl, whilst at the same time, the hamster was going berserk on his Ferris wheel. Nan and Grandad stood there motionless whilst the priest was not only speechless but ashen faced, with sweat pouring down his face. Nan was smoking up a storm looking for the culprit, but I had it on me toes onto the sanctuary of the back grass.

I will never forget the tone of the parrot's laughter and the puffs of smoke emanating from the flat, but then the realization that I would have to go back and get a proper right hand after I had laughed at my grandparent's expense. When I eventually resurfaced, Nan found the whole thing highly amusing, even

16

commentating, 'well it was your grandad's idea to invite him round'.

'Fecking serves him right'.

5

This was a covert mission for launching a career in the gambling business. I knew it myself at this point and getting employment at this juncture only cemented that feeling. I marched to the stadium without a 'Danny LaRue' of what I was letting myself in for. After presenting myself to the guvnor, I was assigned a bar under the main stand, where my duties were to pick up empty bottles and clean out the ashtrays.

I was good little grafter, but this was just a ploy. A covert mission to mask the fact I was there to get a grasp of the dogs. It took me a little time, but I became quite adept at what it took to be a champion, and more importantly, I quickly grasped the odds of betting.

At the tender age of thirteen, I could have given you an answer in a split second to any bet, at any odds between one and five hundred pounds. I liked this game, it was more interesting than school, a lot more fun, and I got paid for being there. As time moved on, I started to get friends to put bets on for me, and as it was only ten pence a stake, it was well within my financial constraints. I was fourteen now and starting to develop into a young man, so on the one occasion I fancied this reverse-forecast and couldn't find anyone to put my bet on, I did it myself.

Armed with a growing confidence, I approached the betting kiosk and stated in a manly voice, "Five and one reverse-forecast for fifty pence please", meaning a one-pound stake which at the time was a note. Without even looking at me, he accepted my bet, took my readies and gave me my tickets.

I never won that race, but overall, my percentage was in the positive. I couldn't get enough of it. Penny-up-the-wall, Greyhound racing and three card brag. It was a steady procession, leading, guiding me.

If a game took a deal of thought and there was an element of skill and readies involved, then count me in. I knew what a deck of cards consisted of, I was familiar with the odds and probabilities. Then I was offered work in a spieler, helping behind the bar and generally being a waiter.

The Spieler

Housed above a hardware shop on the corner of Uxbridge & Godolphin, in '*The Bush*' was the hub of the villainy community. It served beer and shorts but didn't have an alcohol licence. There was never a problem with '*the old bill*' as they knew where all the local gangsters were. They stuck to the rules and so did the boys. It was a big open room with a bar, gaming tables where punters played backgammon, draughts, three card brag and the immensely popular Jamaican game of Kalooki, but on Friday it hosted a seven-card-stud poker cash game. This was my introduction to how things worked on the other side. Immaculately dressed and uber mannerly, I was to discover these gentlemen had rules and proper rules at that. Burberry Mac's, Crombie's, the finest cut cloth from Saville Row, Gabicci's, hand-made shirts from Jermyn Street and to top it off, Lizard and crocodile skin shoes from John Lobb. There was a code around these guys that consisted of, be very well presented, polite, and the most important rule of all – keep your fucking mouth shut!

I loved it from the minute I walked in. The guvnor met me at the door, walked me to the bar and explained what I had to do. I went around with bottles of whatever they wanted, picked up the empties, cleaned the ashtrays and occasionally went on a kebab run which was just down the road. I sat at the side of the room and as soon as someone looked in my direction I was there, eagerly awaiting their order.

There was 'H' a local bully that made his money from debt collecting. Six foot three and built like Stamford Bridge, he wasn't one for profound conversation, but no-one fucked about with him. If you owed money and he came a calling, you paid end of!

Lenny-the-dip was a pickpocket that went to work at Liverpool Street train station, between 7 - 9am Monday to Friday, with most of his readies being made between 5 – 9pm on a Friday evening as all the lagging-boats would saunter home. This was in the days when nigh-on everyone carried cash and Lenny was responsible for the game kicking off at ten pm as he would always turn up with chunks of notes.

Jamaican Bob was the sweet boy on the firm. A walking advert for **Stuarts**, he wore a sovereign ring on every finger and a gold chain around his neck so thick I was amazed he could keep his back straight. It was the funniest thing in the world watching Bob play dominoes. If you have never been a party to one of these games played by Jamaicans, you haven't lived. He would jump out of his seat and scream at the top of his voice '*boombaclart*' before smashing the piece into the table knocking the set-up all over the place. It took five minutes to reconstruct the hand but to them it was fun. If you were an outsider, you'd have thought they were going to have a dust-up, but nothing could be further from the truth. It was just their way.

Then there was Mr. A. who worked in the city in something to do with finance. He was completely out of place, but the boys didn't care as he was *cottralled* (a slang term for chunks of readies) and basically fed the table. 'H' done a little bit of work for him on the QT, so he was covered. A terrible card player he done his bollocks every Friday, but in my opinion, I think he just liked the being around the boys, (on the firm).

Tommy was a bookie. Extremely sharp and always on point. He would take a bet on anything. Horses, dogs, football, but he made most of his cash on the card table. He was a good player but took advantage of the table by offering odds on the colour of the flop. For example, three black or red cards was three to one, or on the turn or the river, the offering was high or lower than the previous card. He made fortunes out of Bob as he explained it was like dominoes. I learned a lot from him as he was always on it. He seemed to know something was going to happen before it did, and I got lucky to have him as my mentor.

Next up was Nick-the-Greek, or the bubble as he was affectionately known. He had a string of cab offices in and around North London and seemed to do very well for himself. He also had a spieler in the Finsbury Park area but was unashamed in his love for the game in 'The Bush'! He was introduced to the game by Tommy who used his services a lot. I didn't know what for at the time, but it soon came to light.

Alongside the owner John, Mr. P. made up the rest of the table. A former policeman, he was now an antiques dealer that specialized in probate. A little too serious for my liking but the boys enjoyed taking his money. He would also furnish the chaps with some useful information about a bit of work and the firm ensured he got a nice drink out of it.

Everything was falling into place, so much so that if I had given up half my jobs, I would have solved the unemployment crisis, but I didn't care because this seemed such a natural fit for me. On my second week the dealer didn't turn up, so I was offered that job, but I had no idea about the mechanics of dealing poker.

"It doesn't matter son, come here and we will show you what to do".

This was a daunting prospect for a fourteen-year-old. With that in mind, and after about an hour of the players sorting out the bets amongst themselves, there was a dispute involving a side-pot that was becoming increasingly contentious by the second. To this day, I don't know what made me do it, but I made a decision that could have got me seriously hurt.

A dispute had developed and was close to violence, when I carefully reconstructed the hand and explained the side-betting. I put it to them that the player to my immediate left won, and two hundred and forty-seven pounds of the side bet with the player to his left getting the rest. It went quiet for what seemed like an eternity, before Tommy finally said,

"I knew I liked the look of that kid, well done son, you're on the firm, ring that other ice cream and tell. him to jog on".

I couldn't believe it. I was aghast and struggling to contain my excitement, as I earned more than forty pounds that night, and began my new career as a dealer. I was learning a skill set of seven-card stud, which in my eyes is a better game than the more popular Texas Hold'em. I love it when I hear commentators, start quoting things like C bet, three bet, four bet, look at the texture of the board etc. Anybody fresh to poker would think there is a new language, but this is just a smokescreen. Get a fucking grip, it is just a game of cards.

The club could be described as interesting to say the least, as the players were what some would describe as somewhat unsavory, but they were never rude or impolite to me, so I turned a blind eye to what went on in the background.

Then, one Monday Tommy was outside my school waiting for me. "Fancy a bacon roll and a cuppa tea?"

"100%"

"Glads?"

"Perfect!"

By the time we walked the three hundred yards to the café, my curiosity levels were through the roof. Tommy starts; "Wanna earn some readies on the side?"

"Doing what?"

"The bag under the table needs to get to Brighton tomorrow!"

"That's it?"

"That's it!"

"How do I get there?"

"Take the rattler. Here's fifty quid!"

"What do I do when I get to Brighton?"

"Someone will be outside the station!"

I finished my sandwich when Tommy looks at me suspiciously and say's – "Don't you want to know what's in the bag?"

"Do I need to know?"

"No!"

"I'll make sure I get it to Brighton!"

"Good kid, be here at four tomorrow afternoon!"

I knew what I was doing was wrong but somehow it felt right. Like I was trying to justify it to myself. I bunked off school and about ten am, I got the tube from 'The Bush' to Hammersmith, changed for the district line to Victoria where I paid six or seven pounds for a child return to Brighton. On arrival a nasty piece of work was in a car outside and gestures for me to get in.

"Did you look in the bag?"

"No!"

"Why not?"

"None of my business!"

We drive away from the station and head to a café on Sydney Street. As we pull up, (Mr, trying to be intimidating) turns around in the front seat and hands me a roll of notes –

"What's your name son?"

"David, and you ain't my dad!"

"I don't know where he got you from, but there's a lot more work if you want it!"

"I'll speak to the man!"

"What's his name?"

"Who?"

"The geezer who gave you the bag!"

"What bag?"

"This fucking bag!"

"Don't know what you're talking about!"

He looks at his driver with a big smile on his face –

"You take care son. Enjoy the readies!"

"I told ya! You ain't my dad!"

As soon as he drove off, I counted three hundred smackers. I skipped to the seafront and had an ice-cream before boarding the train back to London. I met Tommy bang on four at Glad's. "How was it?"

"The ice-cream tastes different at the coast"

"You ever done this kind of thing before David?"

"What thing?"

There was that same look on his face as the Herbert from Brighton. Then he hands me a roll of fivers that came to a hundred pounds. I made the best part of a rofe for a day's work, good money in 1977. "Why did you ask me to do it?"

"I liked you from the moment you sorted the action out on your first night at the spieler"

"I think I knew what I was doing!"

"Considering 'H' was in the hand, that could have gone horribly wrong!"

"I got lucky" –

"Let's not beat about the bush here son" –

"You're not me dad!"

"I can't use the bubble anymore as he's under obbo!"

"Do what?"

"Observation! You're the next best thing"

"Why?"

"No-ones ever going to search you David" –

"Thank you!"

"For?"

"Not calling me son!"

It was the start of a profitable partnership.

If you play big boys' games, you play by big boys' rules!!!

And I played them to perfection.

1. Don't tell anyone what you're doing.
2. Don't give anyone an opportunity to guess what you're doing.
3. Keep your fucking mouth shut!

Disappointingly, however, my nice little earner at the spieler was about to come to an end. There was a big hand developing in a game of hold'em, with a raise from UTG, a call from UTG + 1, an all-in from the cutoff, followed by a call from the original raiser and UTG + 1. The room went deathly quiet as the hand involved 'H' and the ex-policeman. It didn't take long for the banter to start when 'H' threw his car keys in the middle only to be followed by Mr. P. who threw in his wallet.

The third member of the coup declared he had aces, so I ran the hand. The pocket rockets held, with the bully coming second; as I split the pot, 'H' reached into the wallet's face and let him have some unsavory expletives. As he opened the wallet, the room stood in shock as it was not a wallet but a badge holder with a policeman's ID attached. Before anyone could say anything, he shouted, "You're all nicked". They came in all guns blazing, pinched everyone, destroyed the place. The cozzer that lost the hand let me go. He knew I was underage, so I suppose it wasn't worth the paperwork. The antiques dealer was a front for him being undercover as they were looking at this game and all that it entailed. Then he said, "They should have paid me!"

Turns out he got knocked for a bit of work he put them into, which I found odd as that was one of the golden rules.

I loved that job. I was making a lot of money running errands and the like. I would have done it for nothing but that would have raised suspicion. Now, what do I do? Fourteen is such a tricky age for a young man; you are neither a boy/child nor an adult. You think you are a man, but you're not; you couldn't be further from it. I had given up on my studies long ago. If I wasn't playing or dealing cards, or at the dogs, I was delivering parcels to the seaside, which courtesy of Mr. P. ended abruptly six months later, and now I discovered something entirely different:

6

1977 was the breakout year for me as I was starting to understand the mechanics of what it took to be a man. I started growing hair where men grew hair; my bollocks dropped, so my impressions of Shirley Temple stopped. I started to bunk off school. Because of Stuarts, I became aware of fashion, my music taste developed with Roy Ayers, Celli Bee & The Buzzy Bunch, Sweet Thunder, T- Connection, The Olympic Runners, et al. I was a proper soul boy with a wedge haircut. We would frequent Crackers on a Friday afternoon, The 100 Club on Saturday, and The Clarendon on a Sunday evening, followed by The Hammersmith Palais. Peter Francis was the main man in dancing circles as he headed up a firm from Notting Hill, Maida Vale, and Kensal Rise, who used to do this line dance to the tune 'Movin' by Brass Construction. It was a proper sight to behold as about fifty of them were in complete symphony with each other. It was the time of Stix Men, Rude Boys, Rockabilly's, Soul Boys, Rastas, Mods and Skinheads.

It was the release of Saturday Night Fever and John Travolta that changed me. He was everything that I wasn't. He was strikingly handsome; he could chat to girls and the coup-de-grace, he could dance. That movie made me realize it was all about confidence and how you carried yourself, so I developed a don't give a fuck attitude that took me a while to perfect, but I got there in the end.

I was a late starter where girls were concerned, but when you are in your early teens, things start happening below the waist. You are staring out the window at school thinking about the game at the weekend, when out of nowhere, you develop a diamond-cutter. A hard-on so intense it feels like all the blood has drained out of your system and into your cock. You don't know what to do as the bell rings for the end of the tutorial. Do I stand, do I make a scene and hope that it goes away, or do I just accept the fact that it is the most natural thing in the world and take stick from my friends. Fuck it. I'll sit here and see it out.

One of the strangest phenomena around boys of that age is personal sex addiction. There is no football training after school or further studies for them. It is full steam ahead to get indoors for the next session in the art of wanking, a skill set we all become experts of eventually. I always found it amusing when someone called me a wanker in the negative sense because, let's face it, both genders enjoy a good Jodrell.

I was fifteen when I went to the shops and saw her. I was a shy kid, but we knew each other from primary school. It was a little awkward at first, but as I became more confident, the relationship started to develop, leading us to become boyfriend and girlfriend - a fact I was very happy with, but with a little apprehension as I had absolutely no experience of sex whatsoever. You start off heavy petting. What do I do with this hand, what do I do with that? Can I touch this, can I touch that? This is fucking hard work. And sometime later, days, months, years, even decades, you eventually get the hang of it. Hopefully!? The truth that no boy will ever tell you, is the sheer relief of breaking your virginity. You have cracked the seal. So, when the conversation eventually comes round to virginity, which invariably it does at that age, you are not the Herbert telling lies because if you are a virgin at that age, you are in for some almighty stick.

When you lose your virginity, it is a thrilling and somewhat strange experience at the same time, because in the pre-internet, no pornography age, you are not sure what your partner is supposed to experience. You pump away for about three seconds when suddenly you start squirting the most unbelievable amounts of goo known to mankind. There you are, all proud of yourself, thinking what a man you are when deep down your girlfriend is screaming. "Is that it? What the fuck are you laying there looking all smug for? Now get back on and sort me out, or I will tell your friends you have got a very small Hampton, your breath stinks, and you're shit in bed" (which you are). Trust me boys, she may not actually say that, but I am telling you one hundred per cent that is what she is thinking. All these years of thinking you were Don Juan only leads to the realization that you are in fact, a Herbert. Well done you!

I still hadn't been to the careers office because I secretly harbored a desire to work in the gambling world. And then, just when I was losing direction, I got lucky. Time after time, I always seemed to walk into these situations. It is a strong belief of mine that it was meant to be. Once a week, I used to visit friends of mine. The older sister had a boyfriend who lived in the Bahamas. One day, a soft top MG pulled up and some real smooth, good looking, well turned out, deep suntan guy got out of the car to be met by said sister. I wasn't intimidated by this guy, but I was intrigued. Straight away, the conversation turned to careers.

"What do you do"?

"I'm a croupier, I work in a casino in the Bahamas dealing roulette and card games".

"I can deal cards!"

"Blackjack, Punto Banco or Baccarat?"

"Seven-card-stud-poker!"

"In a casino?"

"A spieler!"

"A what?"

"A card club!"

"You mean an illegal gambling den?"

"Yes!"

"For future reference, keep that to yourself" –

"100%" –

"Could you help me get a job in the casino business"?

"I have connections in London that will be able to help you".

"Fantastic"!

"Hold on a minute; do you know Pecky"?

"What"?

"How old are you"?

"Sixteen".

"Unfortunately, you have to be eighteen, but by all means, keep these numbers for future reference as they are always looking for good people".

Talk about disappointment…I was gutted - from hero to zero in seconds. However, the thought of becoming a croupier burned inside me!

27

7

I flitted between jobs, but I wasn't happy.

I was two years into working for a family firm when I got lucky again. I found an Evening Standard and thought I would browse the situations vacant section when I saw an advert that read 'Trainee Croupier's required. Please present yourself at Stringfellow's nightclub in Covent Garden. (Smart dress essential)' I failed to see that last part!

You could barely see my features as I was covered in soot. I leapt out of my seat to look where we were, and it was one stop to Piccadilly. Perfect; I could walk there in five minutes. I disembarked the tube, flew up the escalators, and bound out into the three o'clock Friday afternoon sun.

On my approach my heart sank, as there was a queue a mile long, and as time was precious, I nearly turned around. As luck would have it though, yet another twist of fate would fall my way. There were some slight building works going on inside the club, and because of that, one of the recruitment consultants directed me straight inside. For about ten seconds, I stood at the entrance perplexed until another consultant approached and proceeded to walk me into the kitchen. "How do I apply for a job"?

"What"?

"As a trainee croupier".

"What? Did you not read the ad?"

"Clearly not".

"I am sorry, but you are going to have to vacate the premises".

"No drama, mate. Sorry about that".

Then one of the best voices I have ever heard said.

"What is going on here"?

It was the boss. She stated that whilst I was there, I may as well take the mathematical test: twenty questions and fifteen minutes to do them. The feeling of disgust in the room was highly noticeable. There was an attractive female on my table that would have stabbed me in the face with something sharp if she could. She gave me a look of 'go on, say something and I will fucking destroy you.' I nearly did, too, I thought it was hilarious, but I can assure you no one was laughing about sixty seconds later when I stood up.

The boss came over completely unimpressed.

"Can you sit down and finish the test please. Against my better wishes, I have given you an opportunity, so do me the common courtesy of completing the task".

"I have".

"What"?

I thanked her for the opportunity and attempted to leave.

"Hold on a minute; check that paper".

On inspection, the ice-cream that asked me to leave earlier looked at the paper and presented it to the boss.

"Is this some sort of joke"?

"Do what"?

"You got all the questions correct in less than a minute".

"I did".

At this point, I was not going to volunteer any information surrounding my gambling background as I was completely winning this little scenario.

"Come with me, please. I would like to discuss this further".

We are alone in an office when I started to get some intrusive questioning.

"Do you know people in the business"?

"No".

"Did Pecky give you the answers"?

This was making me a little uncomfortable, so I tried some reverse psychology.

"If you don't want to process the application further, then so be it".

"OK, I tell what we are going to do. Can you come back on Monday washed and presented in a suit"?

"I'll see you Monday".

Those questions were easy – well they were to a settler. It gave me an edge. The competition was fierce, as croupiers were well-paid. I had done this for a living. My immediate thought was job done! Now all I had to do was get cleaned up and hope they liked the look of me.

I spent Sunday in the newly built leisure center on Bloemfontein Road in 'The City' as it had a sauna and all that malarkey in there. The purpose was to get as scrubbed as I possibly could.

Monday morning arrived, I got myself ready in a suit from Reiss, a pair of Bassweejun loafers, and a shirt and tie from TM Lewin on Jermyn Street.

"Where are you going all dressed up"?

"I've got a job interview",

"Doing what"?

"As a croupier".

"What's that"?

"A dealer in a casino".

"A casio".

"No, Nan, a casino".

She just stared at me, pretending she knew what I was talking about.

"OK, love, good luck.".

I checked the mirror and proceeded to make my way to Soho. In terms of my future, there was a lot on the line here. I gave some consideration to what I had done before, and it all just seemed to fit.

I got the tube to Oxford Street, walked southbound down Regent Street, left into Beak Street and into Soho before finishing my journey at Archer Street. As I turned, I saw the lady who asked me to return, so I made my way over, "Hello".

"I beg your pardon".

"I'm David".

"Who"?

"The guy whose face you couldn't see on Friday, you asked to come back in a suit".

"My, my, David; Pecky would be proud".

"Anything would have looked better than Friday".

"OK, let's get the paperwork done".

I gave her my passport for ID purposes, filled out a GB11, and was given a start date for the next training school that commenced in four weeks.

8

Like a Gazelle I bound up the stairs from Piccadilly full of the joys of Spring. I genuinely didn't know what to expect, so, imagine my surprise when a beautiful blonde standing with a map in her hand said, *"Excuse me, do you know Pecky"?*

"What"?

"I'm looking for Archer Street" -

"It's only round the corner. As it 'appens I'm going that way meself".

"Thank God for that!"

We headed north up Shaftesbury Avenue for about two hundred yards, left on Great Windmill Street, and right onto Archer Street. However, I was about half an hour early, so on the corner of Great Windmill Street, I found a coffee shop and directed the young lady where she wanted to go. "Do you mind if I join you"?

"This is a little coincidental, but are you starting the croupier school today"?

"Fuck off".

"So am I",

We made introductions leading us both into relaxing and getting into conversation.

"Did you go to Stringfellow's"?

"Yes, I did".

"It was somewhat busy, wasn't it"?

"You're not wrong".

"Did you find the questions difficult"?

"A little".

I didn't want to seem like a pompous, arrogant prick, and before I could get on to my little tale about my appearance, her face changed, and she got a little angry.

"Well, I found the whole affair irritating".

"Why's that"?

"I was in the process of going through the questions, when some prick fresh off a building site covered in soot, came and sat next to me".

31

"Straight"!

"Ruined my suit...then to make matters worse, he finished the test in about sixty seconds".

"Bollocks"!

"I bet a wanker like him would never get a job like this".

"That would be me".

"What"?

"The prick you are talking about".

I proceeded to give her a breakdown of the short time our fragile relationship had begun and ended when....

"Oh my god, it is you; I recognize your voice now".

It was at this point I suggested we make our way to the casino as the school was about to commence. There was a stony silence as we entered the building - mine from a little apprehension, hers from complete bemusement. I signed in at reception, produced the relevant documentation, and entered the old Golden Horseshoe Casino, which was now in use by the Metropole Group as a training school for would-be-croupiers.

At the start of play we were given a welcome speech by the trainer Maria, where we were informed of how the school was structured; it was 11 a.m. to 7 p.m. Monday to Friday to ensure that in six weeks' time, we had the relevant tools to be let loose in a casino.

During the four-week waiting period, we were furnished with paperwork to learn our 5x, 8x, 11x 17x and 35x tables from 1 to 40 for Roulette purposes. As Maria finished her speech, we were given a test paper of fifty questions with fifteen minutes to complete. After about three or four minutes, some guy from across the room and I stood up at the same time. Approximately twenty minutes later Maria read the scores out - Imogen 31, Sophie 38 etc, before getting to me and declaring 50, the same as the other guy. Maria stared at me with suspicious eyes.

"Can you come with me please, David"?

As we get into the office, the three trainers were waiting for me.

"No one gets those questions right in that time".

I protested.

"What about the other geezer"?

"We know all about him! And another thing if you wish to continue this course, you are going to have to take elocution lessons".

"Elocution what"?

"A course to improve your pronunciation".

My cockney accent was a tad inappropriate apparently. By this point, I had had enough. "This feels like persecution to me".

"Well, those are the rules".

"You know what you can do with your fucking rules, don't ya"!

I stood up and offered my hand,

"You can jog on",

The three of them fell about laughing as it was a getup. When the laughter subsided, I was directed to a roulette table and given ten stacks of twenty chips; then instructed to knock them down and pick them up in the quickest time possible. A pointless task, you may think, but it was essential for manipulating your fingers in how to handle chips/checks.

The word 'lump' is not a derogatory term by any means. It is fitting in describing how a trainee cuts chips, clears a layout, and audibly repeats bets. The difference between a trainee dealer, and an experienced dealer is comparable to all trades in the workplace, whether it be a bricklayer or a waiter. An apprenticeship in any trade takes approximately four years and a lot of exams. A training school was six weeks on one game of which mine was roulette. An example would be when you pass your driving test; it doesn't mean you are a driver. The pass certificate means you are considered safe to drive on the roads. It is the same as waiting tables or dealing in a casino. It takes years to become proficient; however, the structured training we received enabled us to be considered by any casino manager, pit-boss, or inspector safe enough to deal small games at first and then larger one's as you became more proficient.

Again, we were given ten stacks of twenty chips and had to go through what seemed a monotonous but necessary procedure of knocking them down and then 'chipping up.' It was repetitive, but it loosened your fingers to enable you to manipulate the chips/checks. This went on for another hour before we were given another fifty-question test with fifteen minutes to complete them.

We finished about another hour of chipping when Maria announced, "OK, guys and gals, that's it for today. Everyone is invited for welcome drinks at The Lyric pub on the corner of Great Windmill Street".

I was strapped into a conversation with this young lady when the bell goes, "Are you getting a train home"?

"I am".

"You can walk me to the station if you like".

"I'll get me cloak".

"Where do you live"?

"White City".

"Where's that"?

"Shepherds Bush".

"I live miles away from that".

"Where's that, love"?

"Ealing".

It was three or four stops on the train. Being a gentleman, I made the obvious and very unsubtle suggestion.

"Shall I walk you home girl"?

"I was hoping you'd say that".

We passed White City, East Acton, North Acton, and West Acton before arriving at our destination Ealing Broadway.

"Is it walking distance, or shall we get a sherbet"?

"We can walk from here. It will give us a chance to get to know each other".

"How long have you known Pecky"?

"What"!

"Why are you doing this"?

"I met some geezer, who told me it was a good number. You"?

"My fella works on the ships".

"Doing what"?

"In the casino, dumbo".

"I didn't know ships had casinos on them".

"Clearly, I'm gonna do a year or two, and then I'm off".

"OK, I'll have a quick coffee and then call a taxi".

"What"?

"Don't you have a boyfriend"?

"What do you think he is doing on the ships"?

"Ain't got a clue"!

"Hanging out the back of something every night of the week".

"I beg your pardon"?

"You heard".

"And anyway, I haven't had a bunk up for ages, so you are just going to have to put up with me. Or don't you find me attractive"?

I liked this game.

"Good, because I want fucking" –

....

Day 2

The first two hours of the day consisted of knocking down chips and picking them up, and then a fifty-question maths test. The annoying part of the test was attempting to write the answers down with spastic hands. The constant repetitive procedure of chipping up left your hands in a state of shock. The muscles in your fingers were not used to it. The ache subsided after about ten minutes, but it was a very strange feeling indeed.

Even though we were on day two, you could see and feel little cliques forming, so I was delighted when Sophie approached me for lunch purposes. I thoroughly enjoyed her company. She was gregarious, vivacious, and bubbly - As we paid the bill, she had a firm grip on my leg to ensure that I stayed put, so when the other girls left, she asked me a question: "What are you doing this weekend"?

"Playing football on Saturday".

"You were playing football".

"OK, I was: what am I doing now"?

"Mummy and Daddy are away this weekend, so you are coming over to my place".

The rest of the day we spent knocking down stacks, chipping up, and doing maths tests. Seven o'clock came, so it was off to the boozer again. Unbeknownst to me, it was a casino pub that catered for the Charlie Chesters and Golden Nugget crew. Again, in my naivety, I had failed to grasp the concept of the night-time economy.

"Are you two coming to Hombre's"?

"Hombre's"?

"We always go to Hombre's on Tuesdays; it's fifty pence a drink".

"Shall we have a look"?

"Absolutely; what's not to like about fifty pence a drink".

Hombre's D'Bahia was a nightclub based on Adam & Eve Court off Oxford Street that catered for the casino crew of London. Considering there were twenty-eight casinos, you can only imagine how busy it used to get, particularly on Monday and Tuesday. Housed at the door by Andy and DJ'd by the one and only Chelsea supporting top pal of mine **Johnny Norman**, it was my introduction into the midweek nightlife of the West End.

At close to kicking out time during the erection section, I suggested to my dance partner it might be a good idea if we chipped,

"Shall we get a taxi"?

"I'll get me coat".

"Where are you going"?

"White City"

"I didn't know you lived in the city".

"I don't".

Once again, my immaturity came to the fore.

"Why are you going to the city"?

"Do I need to spell it out for you"?

"What"?

"Your mate from last night told me".

"What mate"?

At this point, I noticed the cab driver staring at me open-mouthed thinking, *how much of a fucking idiot are you?*

Day three-and-four were the same as day two in terms of procedure, chipping up, and more maths tests. Amid the daily routine, I could feel the policy working. I was a lot quicker than on Monday, and I was starting to do the tests in double sharp time too; everyone was. Little by little, day-by-day - we were slowly turning into dealers.

Friday arrived so Sophie and I had lunch, walked to Green Park, got a tube to Victoria before boarding a train to the green suburb of Surrey.

I had never been inside a proper country house before, where people wore wellies and Barbour jackets to walk the dogs. In the evening, we went to the local village pub where we had a Ploughman's for dinner, a couple of real ales to wash it down, followed by a glass of port.

I thought about the opportunity that I had been given and knew as long as I showed a keen eye for detail, I would get to work in places that people with my limited education would never get to see. I also took stock of where I was and what I was doing. This wasn't me. My name was David Moynihan, not Farquar Rupert-Doings. I didn't belong here; more importantly, I didn't want to be here. I was completely happy with my lot. A boy of Irish immigrants, dragged up on a council estate, that happened to be good with numbers.

Early in the morning, I was awoken by Sophie walking about looking confused, "What happened to you last night"?

"What happened to you more like"!?!

"I must have dozed off. Did you sleep well"?

"Like a baby. Wet meself twice and woke up sucking me thumb"!

She stared at me with this big grin on her face-

"Can you drop me at the station please love"?

"What"?

"I'm playing football this afternoon"!

"But I thought…".

"Before you say anything, Sophie, I play with my mates every week"!

"I can do better than that".

"What"?

"I'll drop you wherever you want to go".

"Really, Shepherds Bush, please".

"Even better, I'm going to view a flat in Earls Court today. When do you want to go"?

"Now would be good".

We loaded up the Land Rover, got on the A3 for about thirty minutes, took the Roehampton turn off, went through the best-kept secret in London, Barnes, over Hammersmith Bridge and down into The Bush.

As soon as I got in, I rang one of the boys.

"Where the fuck have you been"?

"We had a bit of a party last night at that new job I'm doing".

"What new job? I'll be around in arf our, so you can fill me in".

"Sweet, see you in arf our"!

We played the game, got showered, and headed for the clubhouse - where we ordered drinks and engaged in badinage. This was always my favourite time of the week. You had to be quick, or you would get slaughtered, a real man's environment.

Suddenly, there was a deathly silence, like everyone had fallen into a state of shock, it was Sophie.

"How did you find me"?

This was in no way a protest; I was just curious.

"You mentioned it this morning. Anyway, I have a couple of friends over for dinner, and I was wondering if you would like to join us"?

Sunday came with all the pleasantries you associate with having lunch at a village pub. I was in alien territory here, but she had a way of making me relax. I didn't belong, and I had no desire to. I used to deliberately miss lunch on Sunday as I got bubble and squeak on Monday. You should have seen Sophie and gangs faces when I was telling that story; "Take the leftover's, chop it up, fry till warm, top it off with a fried egg and a couple of slices of black pudding"-

"What's black pudding"?

"The remains of a pig"-

"And you eat it? Sounds disgusting"!

"It's very popular in Ireland",

"I knew there was something wrong with the Irish"!

The hairs on the back of my neck stood up, blood rushed to my face and my muscles tightened.

"What did you just fucking say"?

"Come, come now David, don't be fickle"-

"Do what, I'll give you fucking fickle"!

I leant over the table and grabbed him by the hair and stuck one of my fingers up his nose. Quick as a flash Sophie gripped me tightly, put her arms around me and her face reddened,

"We're leaving"!

In the blink of an eye, we were outside enroute to the house, walking at a fair clip.

"You wanna slow down girl"?

"Seeing you on the brink of a fight has made me extremely horny"!

Back to school on Monday and the realisation training was going to take a more technical course. We went through the usual rigmarole of chipping up, a maths test, and now the real work begins - the fundamental teachings of roulette.

There are 37 numbers on a roulette table 1-36 and zero.

It is a 2.73 house percentage game. Placing one chip on every number = 37 chips. A straight up pays 35-1, meaning you retain 36 chips. You lose one chip in 37 or 2.73 chips in every hundred.

There is a vast.array of bets you can make, such as:

A straight up or one chip on the number pays 35/1

A split, one chip between two numbers pays 17/1

A corner, one chip between four numbers pays 8/1

*A six-line, one chip between six numbers pays 5/1

A street, one chip between three numbers pays 11/1

There are outside bets, which consist of three columns or three dozen that are paid 2/1.

And then there are the even money bets that consist of high/low 1-18, 19-36, red/black or odds/evens, which get paid 1/1. If zero hits, you lose half of your original stake.

There are also various prop bets on the layout, such as:

Tiere, a six-piece bet consisting of,

5-8

10-11

13-16

23-24

27-30

33-36

Voisins, a nine-piece bet,

0-2-3 x 2 chips

4-7
12-15
18-21
19-22
25-26-28-29 x 2 chips
32-35
Orphelins, a five-piece bet,
1
6-9
14-17
20
31-34

We didn't know it at the time, but to compound matters, it was a French wheel with an American layout. There are what I consider the most challenging of bets, Neighbours. It is a five-piece bet consisting of the number you proposition plus the two numbers on either side. It sounds easy on paper, but when you are going through the training process and what gets done first in terms of procedure, is far from easy. At the same time, you calculate how much the bet costs, what change they get and take other bets, all before the ball drops. That is why it takes a long time to become fluid, it takes skill and no little guile to become proficient, and I take my hat off to all and sundry that survive training and go on to become experienced dealers.

We now had to undertake the laborious task of having to do all of this together, keeping in mind we did it devoid of emotion. You can't smile at a person that has just won because, there will be someone sitting next to them that has lost. On the flip side, the same applies to a player that has lost, you can't show sympathy as that could be construed as negative, so you keep your emotions to yourself whilst at the same time being ultra-professional. This was drummed into us. Under no circumstances, were you to enter a discussion regarding a bet, or a dispute? The only word out of your mouth was "Chef". As soon as the inspector was alerted to a potential problem, they dealt with it, not you!

Day 2 of week 2, was the day of reckoning. Gone were the niceties of the previous six days as the professionalism of the training crew kicked in. I was learning a new skill, and I created,

40

forged and established relationships with the trainers as I admired the way they went about their business.

Now we get into weeks three and four and more of the same but with a little more urgency. They were structured by way of learning how to spin a ball, how to make a bet and give change from chips/checks or cash, verbalise it, clear a layout, as well as chipping up, chip cutting, and maths tests.

Week five, we were in the home straight, and delivering the whole process. There would be two-or-three-lumps on one side of the table as players, whilst I dealt and went through the whole concept of delivering a game. From spinning the ball to taking bets, to clearing the layout and paying winners. The taking and calling of proposition bets was easy as I had experience on racecourses; however, what do I do with this hand, what do I do with that was a little confusing. As the days went by, we were all getting a little quicker, but you can now understand why we were called lumps.

We were in The Lyric as usual when I was approached by two ladies who were currently employed at Charlie Chesters -

"What casino are you going to".

"Sorry"?

"What casino have you been assigned"?

"I don't know".

One of the trainers Morien, joined in,

"Probably Chesters"-

"Sweet! You'll fit right in at Chesters"!

"Is that so"?

"Oh, by the way, *do you know Pecky*"?

The last week was a little more training with a lot more emphasis on introducing us into our casino, paperwork, uniform fittings etc, before Friday and the big party. The champagne flowed, a DJ showed, a good time was had by all. In six weeks, I had learned a lot.

It was the persistence to finish the laborious task of knocking down stacks of chips and picking them up that made you a croupier. The constant maths tests, the non-stop drills and exercises. The trainers trying to lure you into an argument you are never going to win that turn you from a '*Lump*' to a dealer. To Bob Borg and his team, Maria, Gary and the ice-cream that is

Morien, I salute you. Thank you for giving me the tools to succeed!

9

Act 1

Charlie Chesters casino was a living breathing organism, throbbing to the beat of a hedonistic nightlife. Home to Roulette, blackjack, punto banco and dice, it provided an itch a gambler needed to scratch.

A pleasure dome of adult pastime unparalleled in London, Soho was dirty, dangerous, sex shops akimbo with a brass aplenty. There were players, spielers, prevalent coke and 'E' dealers. It was a real den of iniquity, but to those of us that worked there, it was a way of life.

Red velvet curtains adorned the walls, the carpet was akin to a front-line trench in wartime, and the smell from cigarettes was overwhelming, but it is without a doubt my favourite place to have had the pleasure to work in. It was the people that made Chesters the best little casino in the world. Jocks, scousers, manc's, paddies, cockneys and a lot of extremely attractive females were the make-up of its soul. I was driven, guided here, from the hard-core gambling street corners of an estate to White City Stadium, to a spieler in 'The Bush', to working the bags on courses. Call it fate, but everything I was good at, was in this little establishment.

Having got myself prepared in black trousers, black waistcoat, white shirt, and bowtie; I joined the rest of the crew in the canteen for my first shift as a croupier. I was six foot three, fourteen stone and had grown up on a very tough council estate. As I entered the fray, I could feel its beating heart, pulsating to the constant turn of a card, the spin of a wheel or the roll of dice.

As it was my first shift, I was tasked with chipping between four busy roulette games, a detail that involved emptying machines with stacks of twenty chips and replacing them on tables that enabled the dealer to keep a constant flow of the game. It was an easy enough exercise, but more importantly, it was an opportunity to watch dealers, and as your experience grew, it gave you the nous to prepare bets for them. However, as this was my first shift, you are a proper hindrance. The dealer is glaring at you, the inspector is shouting obscenities, and the pit-boss would stab you in the face with something sharp if he or she had access to it - a very unattractive proposition for someone of a timid disposition -

A little later, I had come on leaps and bounds. What made me the dealer I became was down to the inspectors. Not only were they firm, professional and insightful, they were helpful as well. They would bellow from their chairs, 'wrong hands, inside hand, outside hand,' and if they had to, they would get out of their seat and show you. In the entire time I spent in the casino business, I never experienced another team like them. It is one of the predominant traits that Chesters was renowned for, and something for which I am eternally grateful.

La Lyric, (In the French Quarter)

Was full to the rafters with young casino boys and girls eager for a night out. Comparatively small in stature, The Lyric public house, was the hub of all things social for lumps. You get to create and forge relationships with a host of new people. Far from being a killjoy in terms of a social life, the vibe was one of flirt and mingle. This suited me down to the ground, so at closing time, we left as a unit and headed for Hombre's and the promise of a shoeshine shuffle. With the legendary *Johnny Norman* and his dulcet tones on the decks, the dance floor was heaving with lumps. You could bump and grind all night safe in the knowledge that you literally couldn't miss.

Whilst I was in the queue for the cloakroom at closing time, I was approached by a female dealer from a previous school.

"Are you David"?

"I am"!

"My pal told me all about you"!

"What pal"?

"From Ealing"

"Oh, that pal".

"Gave you a glowing report".

"I'm a report now, am I"?

"What are you up to"?

"Going home to roll a big fat one".

"Sounds good. Want some company"?

I couldn't believe my luck as I had been eyeing up this girl for ages, so I replied, "Yes, I do"!

This, however, created a dilemma. The girl that I had just spent the entire erection section with was waiting for me upstairs, or so I thought. As I got to the top of the stairs, my escort had her tongue down my pal's throat, dry humping him in the middle of the street. Turns out she was dancing with me to get to him. *Fucking mercenary.* We got back to my place to roll a big fat five-paper cone, when it suddenly dawned on me.

"Bollocks"!

"You're not married, are you"?

"Don't be so ridiculous"!

I was so stoned I hadn't noticed her getting undressed and into bed.

"Girlfriend"?

"No, I'm playing football in the afternoon".

"Well, you had better get in here or you'll be too weak to play"

"Where do you live, girl"?

"North London".

"I'm going to Paddington; I'll walk you to the train station".

"What are you doing after"?

"Dunno! I ain't got any plans".

"Why don't I come and watch you play? It will give us a chance to get to know each other"?

"After last night, I don't think there is a lot left that I don't know about you"!

"Cheeky fuck"!

"You started it"!

"That's it then; I'll come to football, and we can have a few after the game"!

From the kick-off, it was abundantly clear the Italians were a far superior outfit. Some of these boys had played at a senior level, with the flip side being our boys were nowhere near as good. Half time came with us getting beat by chunks, however, halfway through the half time oranges, Mick said to me, "I heard you ain't much kop"!

"That's right"!

"Give it ten minutes; then you can have a run about if you like"?

"Sweet"!

With the game over, I was met outside the changing rooms by my new associate,

"You didn't tell me you could play football".

"I can't".

O'Neill's pub in Shepherd's Market, was right in the heart of Mayfair. Even in the best parts of London, you could find ladies of the night, except here they were rather more expensive. Kathy and I ordered drinks before colleagues of hers were coming over and saying hello as she worked at The International, which used to be the Playboy Club. They maintained a lot of the old protocols, including the shift having to stand on parade before the seamstress to ensure they looked the part before going on the floor. Things were very different in those days; some may say old fashioned, but it was what made the casino business glamorous.

As we made our way out of the park, Mick walked past, so I suggested it might be a good idea if I came for a drink or two as it should help in getting to know the boys. Kathy agreed, and off we went to be met at the pub by what can only be described as a charm offensive.

So, it was with gusto when Peter came over and introduced himself, they got the full-on council estate footballer me. I mean, this was what it was all about. Big Peter Gabbadon was the first to approach, quite cautiously, though, but once we had established that I used to frequent the old shabeens in Hackney, gave us both a chance to dig and delve. Like me, Peter was a big Mighty Diamonds fan who loved soul music too. A big man who was quick on his feet became not only a friend of mine overnight but is still a friend of mine today. I moved on to Mick. He had on his wrist a solid gold watch given to him by Hugh Hefner, the owner of Playboy. It was engraved with the words 'To Mick with love, Hef.' It was his pride and joy and reward for fifteen years continuous service. We get into it about the Hotel and Catering league. He felt with a couple of additions to the squad, we had more than a good chance.

46

My playing for money days were over; I couldn't maintain a job in the casino business, train twice a week, and play on Saturdays. One of them would have to give, so I chose my casino career.

Like a father and his long-lost son, I followed Mick around the room, as I was to discover most of the boys were a lot like me. They too, were meandering through life when a window of opportunity within the night-time economy had presented itself. Their individual circumstances were not too dissimilar from mine in terms of looking for a career. There was Danny and Andy, two doormen from Crockford's, proper shysters who, could mug you right off. There was the Peter, a receptionist at The International. He was a man of Jamaican descent who had a somewhat fiery temper; he would fly off the handle at any given moment, or let's have it right, a very good footballer but a fucking raving lunatic! There was the goalkeeper, invariably named 'the cat' who couldn't catch a cold but was particularly sharp with his tongue. In fact, there were all types that could be considered Londoners I would get to know as the season progressed.

Close to the bell Kathy asked if I fancied the Dover Street wine bar, an establishment considered the Hombre's of Mayfair. We had been on it for about six hours now, and if I wanted to continue in this vein, I would have to get some **hurry up!** I was in conversation enroute to the wine bar with one of Kathy's friends when said new girlfriend declared "I'm off me trolley"!

Ever the gentlemen but with a heavy heart, I hailed Kathy a taxi. I was about to close the door - "What the fuck are you doing"?

"Putting you in a taxi"!

"Get in; I'm coming to yours"?

"Sweet! But first, I need to make a couple of stops".

Clem Attlee Court was my first destination. Based behind North End Road in West Kensington Fulham, it had a notorious reputation. Staunch Chelsea supporting country, it was sweet for me as I had a chunk of pals who lived in the area. However, you had to be careful. Even though it was midnight on a Tuesday, there were plenty of Herberts about, so my mate was a little surprised when I knocked on his door.

47

"What's the matter with you? You're a drug dealer, ain't ya"?
"Do what"?
"I need some sniff".
"On a fucking Tuesday"?
"I got a girl outside".
"How much do you need"?
"Gis an eight-ball!".
He put a little line out for me, went to another room, and returned with the gear.
"Take care, mate"!
"See you later, son"!
Re-charged and fired up, I got back in the taxi.
"Where to now, mate"?
"Blythe Road. Just round the back of Brook Green, please"!
I knock on my mate's door, and he again repeated what my last visit said, "What the fuck do you want on a Tuesday"?
"You got any of them pills"?
"I have"!
"Gis two of 'em"!
"You going on one?"
"Why not"?
"Sweet"!
Back in the cab. "White City, please"!
"The estate"?
"Please"!
"No chance".
"What"?
"Bollocks to that, last time I went there, I got done".
"Do what"?
"Done a runner, so I give chase when I realised there were four of them".
"And"?
"They turned round and gave me a proper hiding. Fucking broke my nose"!
"Any chance you can drop me off at Bloemfontein Road?
"I want the readies now"!
"How much"?
"Eighteen quid all in"!
"Here's an apple; keep the change"!

48

"Sweet"!

Five minutes later, Kathy gave me the third degree.

"What the fuck are you up to"?

"Do what"?

"Don't try to mug me off"?

"What the fuck are you talking about!

"You just took me to the scariest parts of London, what the fuck is going on"?

I went into critical thinking mode. It would have been easy to make up some fanny, but I found myself in a unique situation as by now the cocaine was sinking in. I explained '*it is what it is*'; I had grown up with these people, I was a part of the fabric and I didn't know any different.

"Fancy a tickle?"

"Not yet; roll a joint!"

"Not that sort of tickle, dumbo…a bit of shovel, yayo, cocaine."

"I've never tried it before."

I set it up for her and gave her a rolled-up note.

"Sniff it up through the note."

Cocaine has an enormously beneficial effect on certain neurons in the brain, with the adverse effect being it will get you talking a load of bollocks. You become an expert in debate and discussion, so much so that you will repeat yourself again and again. Kathy and I are two lines in when……

"What else did you get?"

"Excuse me?"

"We stopped at two places!"

"And?"

"I am not a fucking idiot!"

Where I come from, people don't ask questions, '*them's the rules!*'.

"I'm sorry for leaving you alone in the cab."

Then it hit me; I had committed a deadly sin. I would have been easy to spot. These were very-smart businessmen, backed up by heavy-duty gangsters. I knew I had made a rick.

"I'll give you the answer to your question if you promise to forget what happened and where we have been. It could get me into a lot more trouble than I am already in. I'll even give you my favourite anecdote from one of the boys. He goes down to Portsmouth on a bit of work. picks up the gear, before joining the A3 back to London. After about ten minutes, a car pulled up beside him with two geezers - one in the front and the other in the back. The Herbert in the back pulls a gun and instructed my pal to pull over (bad move). They both get out of their respective cars and in the ensuing melee, the idiot. got a proper right-hander. With said receptacle now in my mate's possession, he begins firing it at said Herbert, but it was jammed, enabling the supposed hijacker enough time to escape. Utterly bemused, my pal went home to try and work out what went wrong. He started giving it the once over; when he got to the trigger, he inadvertently pulled it, and a flame came out of the nozzle. It was a fake as it had been turned into a lighter. *A fucking lighter!* He drove round to my house, and I have never laughed so hard in my life. Anyway, the point I was trying to make was you don't fuck about with these guys, end of"!

"OK, I get it; what did you get"?

"Pills".

"What are they"?

"They are new".

"What the fuck are they"?

"E".

"What"?

"Ecstasy"

"What"?

"Doves from the Dam".

"Any good"?

"Let's drop one; you will find out in about ten minutes".

"Sweet".

We poured each other drinks and settled down for a good 'ole Charlie babble. Approximately ten minutes later, the first of the sensations started, quickly followed by waves of euphoria. We were both on our feet proper cutting some rug, when the tactile session started. We danced for about three hours non-stop, a constant orgasm in a pill and if you ask anyone from that era, they will all say they were the best.

We would regularly find ourselves in some crooked gaff, doing something we shouldn't, but it made Soho what it was. This went on for about ten months; then I got some good news.

I was in the changing room when Eddie Aston, the Boxman Dice/Trainer announced, "Which one of you is Monza"?

"Me,' I declared.

"The next dice school starts Monday, and you are on it. It runs for one month, Monday to Friday, from nine in the morning till half one in the afternoon. Don't fucking bother turning up if you are late. OK"?

Act 11

At 8:55 a.m. on a brisk Monday morning, Greg, Ruggsy, 'A' level and I went downstairs for our first day of dice/craps training. We met Eddie full of energy, with smiles on our faces, proud of ourselves because we had been selected for the toughest of casino schools.

However, the reality of what we had let ourselves in for did not take long to work out. After that first day, it was obvious why dice dealers were the loudest and brashest, sharp-tongued and quick-witted.

There are three dealers and one Boxman. There is a stickman who controls the pace of the game, calls the number, pays out any centre action; there are two base dealers who look after the other activities, including front/back line, place, come/don't come etc, and there is the Boxman whose job it is to make sense of all the ensuing madness.

It is without a doubt the greatest game on Earth; on a busy day, there is nothing that comes close to it. The energy generated from a twenty-minute roll or longer is comparable to a local derby.

There are thirty-six combinations of two dice that evolve around the number seven. There are six ways to shoot a seven, and three to shoot a four. That is why four and ten pay 2/1. It is why it is the most popular game in the States because it is the only game that pays true odds.

I was struggling. After we finished the third week, I approached Eddie with the intention of quitting. Eddie was a little taken aback, but said I was trying too hard, like I had a point to prove when all I should concentrate on was practising the procedures. I listened to what he said and followed his lead. I thought about penny-up-the-wall and the deep observation of what made the players excel. I thought about patience, three card brag, poker and a deck of cards. I thought about the dogs and how I had mastered the odds. I thought about the spieler. I thought about the things I was good at before I was sixteen that led me to this point. The correlation between my juvenile gambling career and where I was right now, was there for-all-to-see. It seemed a job as a dice dealer was the obvious next step.

As we finished on Friday, he pointed at me:

"You're on the firm; go upstairs and grab a quick coffee".

No bells and whistles, no congratulations, nothing!

The casino opened at 14:00 p.m. with the dice players filtering in about half-past. The game started, and I did something which impressed the Boxman. A player gave me a chunk of notes; I handed it straight into the middle and declared money change. I waited for the Boxman, who was busy with two other buy-ins from the other side, to give me the amount.

"What's this"?

"Cash change straight out".

He counted the readies,

"Give him a monkey"!

"What's a monkey"?

"A brown hairy thing that swings in trees"!

"What"?

"Just give him five hundred pounds"!

It was the come-out roll, and my guy was the first shooter. He threw an eight, then declared fifteen across, I hand them in the middle, and declare, "In against fifteen across", take two little stacks of one-pound checks, and place his bet of three pounds on each number. The Boxman is off his feet, "How long have you been dealing this game"?

"I finished school this morning"!

"Lying toe-rag. Eddie ain't that good"!

As I stated before, it was in my blood. After break, I was put on the stick.

Being a good stick man is an art, but at this juncture, you are a mess. You haven't got a Danny how to navigate the dice around the table. They land and are placed back in the middle, and there's you looking like a proper ice-cream! Robbo leans over:

"Just cos you and I are out of the same stable, don't go thinking I'm your pal. Now move the fucking dice".

You should have seen the state of me; I looked like a lizard on acid as my tongue was sticking out, and my body got into all sorts of strange positions. For the first couple of rolls, Robbo handed them to the player as it was easier, and as craps is quick, it kept the players happy. Picture this, facing you are two base dealers and a Boxman; in front of them are approximately sixteen to twenty players all trying to vie for your attention at the same time. Do the math!

The action began to die as the players started to lose their money, meaning it was manageable even for a lump like me. John calls me over.

"You're in tomorrow at half one"!

"Do what"?

"You've made the crew son. You're on their rota. Your days off are Sunday/Monday".

Cocaine was now becoming more mainstream as the lines of supply were becoming easier to route, if you'll excuse the pun. I could get sniff from a pal of mine at about eighty per cent pure or higher, but in Soho at the weekend, what you got was ten per cent, and the rest was chopped with various cutting agents, including novocaine, baking soda or even baby laxative. That is why many people have a line and fly in the bog to have an Eartha Kitt. It's all in the laxative.

We had a couple more lite ales, said our goodbyes, before I set out on a journey home. About midnight, the phone rings,

"It's Kathy".

"Hello, you".

"Open the door. I'm outside".

What a sight for sore eyes she was and with a couple of bottles of wine too. I had forgotten about the upside, The great thing about Kathy was that she was not interested in a relationship, just pure unadulterated sex, so after a very good night, we said our goodbyes. I went to Oxford Street and walked down Regent Street, through Soho and into work.

When Saturday Comes!

Day two of my dice career could not have gotten off to a better start; as I walked into the break room, I was met by a catalogue of betting slips and bookies pens. Two young guys were in the corner dissecting the day's football whilst watching Football Focus when one of them came over.

In those ninety seconds, I discovered what the makeup of a dice dealer was. Confident, brash, even salesmen like, the basic principles of what you needed to survive in this environment. It was a man's game played by men, no quarter given, none taken.

There was no-one quicker than me at working out the bets. I was starting to enjoy myself when it was my turn on a busy base. We come out on the point of ten, and so it begins. Chips and checks fly at you from every angle at the same time, with players asking you to place their bets. In against five-pound forty across straight out, in against eight-pound eighty the insides spot one, in against fifteen across spot two, five-pound coming five pounds the hard way ten, spot three, three each the outsides one pound the hard ten next to me, twenty-two the insides spot seven and twelve each the six and eight next to him. Approximately thirty seconds after the last roll, the dice are passed to the same shooter who throws them down the table and the whole process starts again. This was my life for the next year. A voyage of discovery creating new and lasting relationships. A never-ending quest for knowledge surrounding all things dice and casino. I struggled for the first eight months and to be fair it takes years to deal it proficiently but at Chesters and in Eddie, Robbo and George I could not have been trained better.

Thursday night, George was sitting in the corner of the break room minding his own business when......

"Do you know Pecky"

"Who"?

"Geoff Peck"?

"No, mate".

"That surprises me as you remind me of him"!

"Sorry, mate, can't help you".

"I'm sure in time you will get to meet him"!

"Does it take long to get a grasp of this game"?

"Years, however, this is probably one of the better places to learn as there is consistent action, and the box men keep on top of you regarding procedures".

"Good to know".

"You'll be sweet, Monz, trust me"!

Chesters was renowned throughout London as a place where you cut your cloth and moved on. The fundamentals of policy, procedure and camaraderie were second to none. And so it came to pass that after a year of dealing Dice and two years of Soho, it was my time. I didn't plan it this way. It just happened. –

Act 111

I was on the lookout for some flights to 'Beefa' (Ibiza). On a typical April morning after a bleak winter, I went in search of the nearest Travel Agent. We didn't need accommodation as I could sort that, so the first quote of two hundred pounds was too expensive. I went to the Bush but couldn't find anything, so the next course of action was to get an Evening Standard where they had a cheap flights section. It was early, so I headed up Holland Park towards Notting Hill because I fancied a coffee in Hyde Park.

Enroute, I bumped into a pal of mine when invariably the conversation got on to Miami Vice. It was a programme about two vice detectives (Crockett & Tubbs), the coolest show on television by a country mile. Don Johnson, the star of the show, was the epitome of chic, vogue, with a crocodile on his boat for fuck's sake. It was the talk of the town. We all harboured secret desires to be him, so with my spirits lifted, I bound up the hill spotted an Evening Standard van delivering to a local shop and purchased a copy. In the nearest coffee-shop I could find, I ordered a drink, opened the paper, found the flight section and rang a couple of numbers, *nothing!* I was on the brink of giving up and even thinking about a package holiday somewhere cheap and cheerful when I decided to have a look at the Situations Vacant section. At the bottom of the page on the right, almost tucked away in small writing, read an advert. 'Miami, Dice Dealers, ring this number'.

I stared at it for at least five minutes before I managed to gain control of my emotions. I had dreamt of going to Miami ever since that programme had started, and as I was a dice dealer, that advert was aimed at me. This was in the days before mobiles, so I was outside Hyde Park before I finally found a phone box. With my heart pounding, I made the call.

"Hello", said she with an American accent that made it all the more real!

"My name is David Moynihan, and I am ringing in response to an advert placed in the Standard today".

"Do you deal dice, David"?

"Yes, I do."

"Can you come along for an interview today"?

"Where"?

"The Embassy Hotel, Bayswater".

It was in the stars; I was looking at it!

"I am across the road, but I am not suitably dressed for an interview"

"Don't worry, just come over, and we'll make a decision once you've had your interview".

I didn't have enough time to think. I crossed the road, went into reception, located where the interviews were being held and got in the lift. On arrival, I noticed there were about forty or fifty interviewees dressed up to the nines, and there's me in a pair of oxblood Bassweejun's with no socks, Bermuda shorts and a pink Lacoste.

After about ten minutes, the door to the conference room opened, and out came a mid-thirties blonde in a business suit. In an English/American accent, she announced, 'can you all go into the room please'. As I approached the entrance, she put her arm out,

"Not you, David, come with me".

I followed her into a little side room, where we were joined by two of her colleagues.

"What do you know about Miami"?

"Not a lot".

"What do you know about ships"?

"Not a lot"?

"Do you want this job, David"?

56

"Are you looking for dice dealers"?

"Good answer"!

"Then I am your man"!

"How much notice do you need to give"?

"A week".

"Good, couple more questions. Do you wear socks"?

"At work? Yes"!

"What about underwear"?

"I beg your pardon"?

"Well, you are going for that whole Don Johnson, Miami look, seeing how he doesn't wear underpants. Do you"?

With that, I noticed that one of her colleagues was taking a more than keen interest in this conversation. She didn't take her eye off me and was biting her lip.

"Yes, I do, but only at work"!

"OK, I'm happy. What about you girls"?

"More than happy".

"Have we got your number"?

"No!".

"Would you like to work for us"?

"Yes, I would".

"Good, welcome to Atlantic Associates. Kelly will give you the details you need to complete in terms of relevant visas, and I will call with your flight schedule".

"That's it"?

"See you in Miami"!

It is fair to say that I got lucky, so much that the female who was giving me the eye stood up with a big smile on her face, gave me a nod and a wink,

"See you in Miami, David"!

Boom! I went out to get tickets to 'Beefa' and came back with a one-way ticket to the promised land.

You couldn't make it up!

I needed a drink, so I found the nearest boozer and settled down for a few lite ales. I thought about my life and how much it had changed for the better in the last two years. I thought about Nan & Grandad and how thankful I was. I started thinking about London, Shepherds Bush, Hammersmith, Fulham, Chelsea, Notting Hill, Soho, Regent St, Carnaby St, Kings Rd, Leicester

Sq, Trafalgar Sq, Piccadilly, double decker's, the underground, black taxis, Johnny Moke, Stuarts, Chelsea Football Club, dark at half-past three, proper clobber, football, fish and chips, shepherd's pie, Sunday roast, pie and mash and the most important thing of all, sarcasm. I thought about Chesters and the blinding crew I was going to leave. Eddie, Robbo and George, Kerr, John and Phil, the Inspectors whom I shall never forget for as long as I live and everybody else associated with that team, especially Brian Kierans. In just two short years, I was given a lifetime of special memories. The only issue now was how to tell my girlfriend.

I got home about nine with a message on my phone. I got through to Lesley,

"Do you have a pen, David"?

"I'll get one".

"Flight B126 to Miami at 9am on Thursday the 28th of April".

"Got it".

"Once you have secured the relevant visas, you need to call us back to let us know you are coming. OK"?

"Will do".

"OK, once again, see you in Miami next week".

Short, sharp and sweet. Now it was real. I called my girlfriend straight away.

"I couldn't get tickets to Beefa".

"Never mind, we'll go somewhere else".

"I'm going to Miami".

"When"?

"Next Thursday".

"For how long"?

"At least a year".

"You fucking cunt".

"I thought you'd say that".

I contacted my family and told them I had some good news. We sat down for dinner at seven, and I informed them of my intentions. My sister sniggered, "bollocks, who do you think you are? Don Johnson?" My mate just stared at me with his mouth open, and nan couldn't stop smiling. "Bring me back a stick of rock?" My message didn't come across quite correctly, so I implied I wouldn't be back for about a year.

I wanted a look at what the US of A had to offer, from New York to California. For the next week, it was all about preparation. I had to do some research about Florida as the real Miami was not what we perceived on television. We were far from being connected to the internet in those days, so the only information I could locate was from Travel Agents. It would be the start of a completely new chapter, and I was excited. On the morning of the flight, we said our goodbyes. Then they called my name over the tannoid system.

'David Moynihan to Gate 26'.

10

As I boarded, my first thought was the immense size of the plane. You turn left to business and first, or into an area so vast it made you wonder if this thing could get off the ground. I was shown to my seat, and as the flight was relatively quiet, I had the three side aisle seats to myself.

Now we are in the air, the light for the seat belt sign goes off, and quick as a flash, cabin crew with a tray full of champagne approach,

"Glass of champagne, Sir"?

"My name's David".

"Helena. Glass of champagne David"?

"Don't mind if I do. Is this normal"?

"Is what normal"?

"Champagne"

"No, the flight is not that busy, and as we poured so many, this is just a bit of excess".

"Lucky me".

"If you like champagne. Let me know if you want some more".

After another couple of glasses, I had a little snooze then I was awoken by the same lady with a menu.

"Meat or vegetarian"?

"Meat".

"I thought you'd say that".

"Sorry to be so predictable".

"We'll see about that".

"I beg your pardon".

"How long are you on holiday for"?

"I'm not".

"What do you do"?

"I'm a casino guy".

"A what"?

"I'm a dealer".

"You're a croupier"?

"I am".

"You going to work on the ships"?

"How did you know that"?

"We get a lot of the guys on here that do that. What ship"?

"Scandinavian Sun".

"The Sea Escape, we've been on that".

"What's it like"?

"You will absolutely love it".

"Sounds good".

"Are you staying at The Marriott on Bayshore Drive"?

"I am".

"When do you join the ship"?

"I have a couple of days to acclimatise".

"OK, cool, why don't you join me and the girls tonight"?

"Sorry"?

"We stay at The Marriott too. Meet us in reception at nine, and we'll show you Miami".

"Sweet"!!!

With my order for lunch taken, she left with the biggest smirk on her face I have ever seen in my life. Dinner came and went. I watched a couple of movies, then the majestic tone of the captain announced, 'Please fasten your seat belts. We are beginning our descent into Miami'. I got tingles down my spine.

It was the end of April, and uncomfortably hot. As soon as I got outside the air-conditioned airport and in the queue for a taxi, it hit me. I had enjoyed European Summer holidays in various locations, but nothing came close to this. We had endured a particularly nasty winter where it had been cold for about seven months. The driver opened the boot,

"Where are you going, guy"?

"The Marriott, Bayshore Drive, Biscayne Bay, please".

We head south on the I-95, and fifteen minutes later, we arrive. I don't know whether it was the heat, nerves, adrenaline, or excitement, but I was sweating like a convicted rapist. At the check-in, I produce my passport, get my room key, pass the circular bar in the downstairs foyer, get to my room and let out a huge sigh of relief. It must have been the weeklong build-up, the expectation, the survival of a ten-hour flight, all the ambiguity in terms of what I had let myself in for. I lay on the bed and fell into a deep contented sleep.

I woke up a couple of hours later, skipped into the shower and tried to contain my excitement. In typical London Summer clobber, I got in the lift ready to let Miami *ave* it. Located on the ground floor was a bar called Tugboat Annie's that was a regular for people on the ships. I approach the bar, order a drink and ask for a menu when I am asked if I would like to sit at the bar or find a table. All done with an overtly friendly professional attitude. My immediate thought was the guy who served me must be a rear gunner because he was way too amenable. A couple of minutes later, a waitress came over to take my order, and she was even more flirtatious than him, then the penny dropped. This is how they do service in the States, they work you for tips, but they do it with sincerity. I have been in the service industry most of my working life, and I contend today that if you desire to work in this business, then go to the US of A and see how it is done. They are on a different level. She dropped my pitcher off and asked me if I was ready to order,

"May I have a large meat feast pizza, please"!

"You want a large one"?

"Yes, please"!

"How many of you are eating"?

"Just me".

"And you want a large one"?

"Yes, please".

"OK, but don't say I didn't warn you".

I found it a bit odd because I could easily demolish a large pizza complete with a couple of sides in less than ten minutes. But this is the States, and they do things very differently. Five minutes later, she came back with what can only be described as a pizza of humungous proportions. It must have been at least thirty inches with half a cow and three chickens on it. I sat there speechless before attempting a remark that she must have heard a thousand times,

"I didn't realise".

"Obviously, but you asked for it".

"I'm from England, love".

"We have all got our crosses to bear. Is there anything else I can get you"?

"Jug of water, please".

"Oughta"?

"Water"

"Oughta"?

This continued for a minute or so before an English guy sitting at the bar howling his bollocks off came over and told me they didn't understand our accent.

"You have to say waddeeerrrr".

"Why didn't you say that"?

I ate two slices, finished the pitcher, and ordered another. I was sitting at the bar now in conversation with Stud, the barman. Yes, that really was his name when he asks the obvious, "How long you in town for"?

"I'm not sure. I have a nine-month contract on the ships".

"Which one"?

The Sea Escape".

"No way, man, they are great fun, go to the Bahamas for the day, do a bit of shopping, go to the beach or even to the casino. You will love that".

"For how long"?

"It's a day gig, man, you leave at half nine in the morning, and you are back in Miami at around nine-thirty at night, trust me, man, you'll have a blast"!

I liked the sound of this, so I ordered another pitcher.

"Hey Stud, can I ask you a question"?

"Ask me"

"This is my third, and I don't feel a thing. Is it my adrenaline"?

"You English guys are all the same. American beer on draft is only two per cent, so you can drink this piss all night long, and not get loaded"!

"Two per cent"?

"Yeah, man"!

"Fuck that".

"Leave it to me. I'll make you something that will hit the spot".

"Thank you".

Whilst Stud was mixing my drink, I had an opportunity to survey the outside world, and what I saw was what I had imagined. We were in a harbour filled with boats, so I took some tentative steps outside into the furnace that is Miami. Big boats with big people with even bigger personalities. This was a bit of me. In a fleeting moment, I grasped why Americans are brash, and confident. They are very different from us in their approach, but I liked them from the off. I paid my bill and went to my room to prepare for the evening's festivities.

I had a Bayview room, which gave access to the city's best views. Directly below was the A1A or the Macarthur Causeway that ran directly through to South Beach. It is the highway they use in movies giving exposure to cruise ships. I was on the twenty-third floor, and being blessed with twenty-twenty vision, I got a soda, sat on the balcony and let it all soak in.

I was relatively well-travelled, but nothing prepared me for this. I jumped in the shower, put on my best trendy London clobber and went to meet the girls. As I neared the bar, Helena (cabin crew) made a tentative approach,

"Are you David"?

"I am".

"You look nice".

"Thank you".

"Come and meet the girls".

Introductions made and with fresh drinks in our hands we surveyed the bar.

My first impression of the crowd was 'Hispanic'. You could have been anywhere in South America as everyone was speaking Spanish. It was a much older crowd, too, with the guys dressed in Suits and their female companions in dresses or ballgowns. I finished my drink when Helena came over,

"We're going".

"Sweet."

We drove over the causeway, down through the beach area and stopped at the bottom of 14th and Ocean, enroute to The Clevelander Bar and Hotel, which had a bar out front, and a DJ spinning decks in the foyer. Whilst on the way there, I scoped the surrounding area. I had done Ibiza, Majorca, Crete in the summer, but this was a whole new vibe. It was electric. Everyone was smiling, bouncing. Helena looked at me,

"What do you think"?

"Fantastic"!

"Let's get a drink".

The first thing that stood out was the average age of the clientele. In England, I frequented pubs and clubs where most people were roughly the same age, give or take five or ten years. Not in Miami. There were couples dancing that were over fifty, as well as twenty-five, thirty etc. Immaculately dressed and moving to a samba beat, South Beach Miami was run by Cubans and man can they move. Both males and females take great pride in the way they dance, and to watch them gyrate on a dancefloor is erotic. If Americans want to express themselves through dance, they just get on with it. I loved that about them because I could dance. Then Helena pipes up,

"Wanna dance"?

She didn't stand a chance! I just copied what they were doing, all gyration with my hands everywhere, it was a licence to dry hump someone on a dancefloor, and she loved it.

"Fucking hell"!

"What's up"?

"You're very pleased to see me".

"I find the whole thing intoxicating"!

"You find it something! Because you've got a stick of rock in your pocket".

"Walk in front of me to the bar, and I'll get us a drink."

With a fit of giggles, we got another drink then it hit me. Romance, I am an incurable romantic. It was the setting. South Beach with its neon lights, big cars, and Latin beat amounted to a movie scene.

"Let's find another bar".

"I was hoping you would say that".

We made our way South to the bottom of 9th and Washington, turned right and about a hundred yards on the right-hand side found an intimate little Cuban establishment.

"What do you think"?

"Of Miami"?

"Yes"!

"Class"!

"Good choice of word".

"Can you take me somewhere that has live music"?

"I know just the place".

65

Tobacco Road was on the Southwest side of the city in Brickell City. It was the oldest bar in decades and catered for absolutely everyone. There was no dress policy, just good old fashioned live music with the place hopping to a jazz band. This is what I had come to Miami for. *This!* It was as perfect an American bar as you can picture. We made ourselves right at home. We were boogeying away when one of Helena's colleagues appeared with her boyfriend.

"Hey David, this is Stud". The barman from Tugboat Annie's.

"Small world, ain't it"?

"You don't fuck about"!

"I was on the same flight".

"You wanna drink"?

"Yeah, man".

It was the start of a relationship that would end in tears.

"Wanna bump"?

"Don't mind if I do"!

Stud introduced me to a bullet snort sniffer originally used for snuff, a very handy little tool. This little contraption made it quick, clean and crisp. The band was really rocking. People were on the bar, tables, chairs, anything where they could be seen and make some noise. Helena and I were all over each other as the class A kicked in. Even though it was an open-air bar, it must have been at least twenty-five degrees because the four of us were drenched in sweat. Helena had that look in her eye, "Shall we go"?

"Absolutely"!

Back at the hotel, Stud and I say our goodbyes. I thank Helena for a wonderful night and made my way to the elevators. I got into bed and fell into a sleep of coma proportions.

The sound of the phone woke me up.

"Morning".

"What time is it"?

"Half eleven".

"Bollocks"!

"Meet me downstairs in reception at twelve. I'll take you for lunch".

"Sweet"!

When Helena and I set off, we went past Bayview and what was going to be the new shopping centre Bayside, through downtown to Brickell City before reaching Coconut Grove. To this day, it is my favourite place of the US to visit as it is the epitome of what I imagined. After lunch, we did some shopping. I bought some shorts, a couple of polos, and a pair of boating shoes, de-rigueur a la Miami.

"What do you fancy"?

"South Beach".

"We'll grab a coffee and do some people watching".

"Fantastic"!

We were in an establishment at the bottom of 8th and Ocean in the days before it became News Cafe. My radar was on full scope when out of the blue, it struck me. It was old. Not in a trendy way, but in a tired, needs a lick of paint kind of way. There were many old white Jewish people, but the beach area seemed to be predominantly populated by the Hispanic community.

"It looks a lot nicer at night-time".

"I like it in the day. It's gritty".

"I was expecting something a little better".

"You mark my words. It won't be long before this place takes off".

It was 1986, and we were still at least a year away from the first bricks of renaissance that turned Miami into the number one trendy spot it has become. Right now, though, it was not the most pleasant of sites.

The evening was drawing in, so we made our way along the art deco area of Ocean Drive. Even though it was Saturday, I suggested a lite ale at Tugboat's with Stud.

"Hey, guys, what you having"?

"I fancy a cocktail!"

"Me too".

"Make us a Stud special please, mate"!

"Two Stud special's coming up".

Tugboat Annie's had floor to ceiling windows about twenty-foot high that overlooked the harbour, it was sundown, and the gleam off the water made a real picture-postcard scene. I was in the moment when Stud interrupts,

67

"I don't know if you would be interested, but there is a guy at the bar that works on your ship. Real nice guy. I think he's the casino boss".

With nothing to lose and the wind between my sails, I made an approach.

"Alo mate, you don't know me, but I'm joining the Scan Sun tomorrow in the casino department".

"Are you Monza"?

"I am"!

"Alo mate, I'm Ronnie Lee".

"Nice to meet you, Ron. Would you like a drink"?

"No thanks, I'm with my girl, and we are just leaving".

"See you tomorrow".

"Take care".

"Before you go, Monz, do you know Pecky"?

"No, mate"!

I had an early start, and even though it was Saturday night, I wished Helena all the best, thanked her for a lovely day and said if I saw her in the future, I would buy her a drink.

"Fuck that".

"Sorry".

"We aren't going to be friends".

"Well, I thought..."

"You can say goodbye to me in your room..."!

There's a lot to be said about reverse psychology. If you are subtle enough with just a hint of suggestion, it works every time.

11

Full of sausage, bacon and eggs, I squeezed my nervous, excited self into a taxi and directed the driver to The Port of Miami. I had enjoyed the previous two days immensely, but now it was time to get down to business.

There weren't many ships in the dock as it was a Sunday but, sandwiched between two mid-size boats was mine. I stared at the name painted on the side for ages, hoping amongst hope this was not it. 'I've been robbed'. That's not a cruise ship. It's a filthy nightmare. It was nothing like I thought it would be. My dreams shattered in an instant. 'It's a lifeboat at best', and I can assure you if that boat was sinking, we were fucked. If someone had offered me a ticket home, I would have bitten their handed off. What a dump. And that was just the start.

I was early, so I embarked through reception, did immigration, and was escorted to my cabin. As the door opened, I was met with a smell akin to a sewer. The undersized shoebox masquerading as a cabin reeked of old underwear, body odour and shit, which could be explained by the fact my cabin mate was in the process of having said dump. I was appalled. My nice little life in London was a distant memory as I distinctly remember telling my grandmother how life in Miami and the Bahamas would grant me insight into how the rich and famous lived, but then the reality was staring me in the face. Never in a million years did I envisage this when I read the advert, 'Miami, dice dealers required'.

I entered said cabin. On the left was the toilet-shower room, and I use the word *'room'* lightly. Attached to that were the bunk beds and on the right-hand side was some sort of contraption that was supposed to be a wardrobe that had overspill from my cabin mate, complete with black-rimmed filth on shirts, undercrackers with skid marks and socks that smelt like they had been worn a thousand times without being washed. It was about four feet wide and was in desperate need of a fumigation.

I deposited my kit on the top bunk. The longer serving crew members get the option of choice, and it is always the bottom bunk for drunken and bunk up purposes. I didn't unpack because, at this point, I was only going to do one cruise. I hasten to add that one cruise was a day trip to Freeport, Grand Bahama, which consisted of departing at nine-thirty, arriving at approximately twelve-thirty, departing Freeport at six-thirty and back in Miami at roughly ten o'clock. In my mind, I'm thinking I'll have a look and then I'm orf.

The door to the bathroom opens,

"Alo mate".

I never said a word. I just stared at him.

"It's a shithole, ain't it!

Again, not a word.

"Got here yesterday myself. I haven't had a chance to clean yet".

This was better.

"Alex".

"Monza".

"If you go upstairs, there's a little dining room that caters for us. Get something to eat and a coffee, and I'll join you in a couple of minutes. As you can see, it is a little bit cramped for two big fella's".

I navigated my way up two flights of stairs and found the Officer's mess just behind the purser's desk filled with lots of people dressed in white and what looked like casino uniform.

I managed to find a seat by a porthole and survey the crew. Young, tanned, fit with bundles of energy. This was what Helena was talking about when she said I would love it. She wasn't talking about the car crash that is the Scandinavian Sun. She was talking about the crew, my shipmates. A blonde, all white teeth and, well, you know, sits down in the only available seat next to me.

"Hi, I'm Trine".

"David".

"You're the new casino guy".

"That's right".

"I thought you were called something else; don't you have a nickname"?

"Big-knob".

I never said that.

"Monza".

"Oh, you're Monza".

"What does that mean"?

"I believe you know a good friend of mine. I spoke to her last night, and she asked me to keep an eye out for you".

"That's nice".

"Apparently, you worked together at a casino in London".

With that, the door flies open, and Alex asks me to get ready for work as we have set sail and the casino opens in about twenty minutes. According to American law, any casino or considered retail facility can only open in international waters, which is roughly about six miles out or conversely when the pilot exits the ship, which gave us approximately fifteen-to-twenty minutes to get the tables ready. The casino consisted of one dice/craps table, one American Roulette, six blackjack and a hundred and fifty slots/fruit machines.

The Scandinavian Sun was launched in 1968. It weighed 11,979 tonnes, was 440 ft long and carried 1200 souls, including crew. By today's standards, it was literally not much bigger than a lifeboat. The casino was based on deck 4 of 5, and its itinerary was a day trip from Miami to the Bahamas every day.

I flew up the stairs for my first look at the casino, and to be fair, I was pleasantly surprised. Not by the machines and tables as a dice table is a dice table but by the team. In England, once you have gained experience, the mechanics of a working social environment in a casino are extremely negative. I am not entirely sure if that reflects on us as a people, but casino employees love to moan. If there was an Olympic competition in moaning, the casino business would win gold by a country mile. We couldn't accept tips back in the eighties, so there was no motivation to go that extra mile, but I thought that was a get out. Personally, I had come from a building site digging holes to working inside in the warm, getting fed for free and working with as much good-looking fanny as you could handle. I mean, what's not to like.

I walked in to be met by Ronnie with a big smile on his face.

"Dice table, please, Monz".

Sweet, I was on the crew for the day.

As I made my way through the tables, everyone said good morning, with the bonus, they meant it. I got to the craps table, and the same thing occurred. Introductions are made, the checks are brought, checked and counted, and I get a crash course in the difference between American and English dice. The fundamentals of how the game is dealt are the same in terms of what bets get worked first, but the pay-outs, differ slightly, and the minimum check is a dollar, where at Charlie Chesters, the minimum check was ten pence, in essence meaning it was a lot easier to deal.

Ten minutes later and the doors open to a throbbing crowd. It was Sunday, the busiest day of the week, so the table was full in no time. Big bad Red, was on stick and doing a sterling job of selling the game. Red passes the dice to the shooter on the come out who throws a seven, 'winner, winner, winner chicken dinner' cries Red to a chorus of cheers and high fives, even the crew were smiling. The key to this was working for tips, a completely different form of engagement. This was fun, electrifying. In that one roll of the dice, I had completely forgotten about the living arrangements, as I wasn't going to spend that much time in there anyway.

The trip to Freeport took roughly three to four hours, depending on conditions, I grabbed a coffee on my first break and went to the back deck, where a bar was serving drinks and a steel band were playing typical Caribbean music. The sun was shining, there wasn't a cloud in the sky and the ocean resembled a bath. I sat there thinking, 'I'm getting paid for this when two young ladies' approached.

"Are you from the UK"?

"No love, I'm from London, it's in England"! The old territorial instincts kicked in.

"Man, we dig your accent"!

So, it was true, I had heard the stories, but I thought they were bollocks.

"What do we do when we get to the Bahamas"?

"Believe it or not, girls, this is my first trip, but I could make some enquiries for you".

"I don't know what you said but say it again".

The two of them were captivated.

"This is my first trip, so I was going to take advantage of the weather".

"Cool, do you mind if we join you"?

"Of course, not"!

"Wait for me when we get there, I'll come and find you".

"OK cool".

With that, I went back on the stick to a pulsating dice game.

"Didn't take you long".

"This game is a lot easier to deal than at home".

"I wasn't talking about that".

Ronnie made a sideways glance.

"It's always the same with you wrong'ns. You take one look at your cabin and quickly develop an exit strategy. Then you come to work, and fifteen minutes later, you're happy as a pig in shit".

"That's a bit strong, Ron".

"What bit"?

"Calling me a wrong'n".

"It's not aimed at you personally, but you mark my words. You will be out every night on the sauce, bang on the gear, slipping into a nice piece of skirt".

"Sounds like a young man's dream".

"It is but beware of the pitfalls. It won't be your fault either".

"What do you mean"?

"It's the accent".

"What"?

"American women have a big thing for our accent, drives them round the twist, I mean, look at those two birds you were with outside, if she keeps on staring much longer, she will be fucking dribbling"!

All of this said while we were dealing a game, which I found strange as none of the clients said anything. Ronnie then finished with,

"Don't worry about it. They don't understand us".

We are now on our approach to Freeport, Grand Bahama when Ronnie says,

"Don't worry about locking the game up. Go and have a look at the Bahamas".

"Sweet"!

An old saying goes 'once you have seen one palm tree, you have seen them all' in reference to the islands of the Caribbean, but that first time is captivating.

I found the girls, got a taxi and directed the driver to Xanadu beach, about a ten-minute drive from the port. This is the life. I strolled on to that beach like I owned the gaff.

We swam, drank, frolicked all afternoon. The setting was beyond perfect. I had my first experience on a jet-ski. I had been in Miami for two days and the Bahamas for an afternoon, I don't think I could have gotten off to a better start. We get back to the ship via a quick drink in Pier One, and I arrange to meet the girls at some point later. I get to my cabin, and the reality of a day/cruise/ferry ship life hits me, (the smell).

"I don't think this is very funny".

"Which part"?

"Are you serious"?

"I don't know about you, but I am loving life".

"To be honest, I was expecting a little more"!

Alex made me realise we could clean the cabin. We would not get any privacy because of the conditions, but you expect that on a ship. I was still on my initial outing, so I was unfamiliar with how things worked in Miami. I made a note to myself that I would not make any rash decisions regarding alternative employment. With my stomach full of a hearty meal, we get to work. The ship was buzzing with day-trippers, keen to impart their experience of Freeport. Everyone is so friendly. I pop to the lounge to watch the band. The audience is captivated, the dance floor is full, the bar is two-deep. This is the reason both Helena and Stud gave the 'Sun' the thumbs up. You go international for roughly twenty-five to thirty dollars. It was a good day out. Work was so busy it flew by when Ronnie closed the game. Big bad Red, invites me for a drink. We have about half an hour to mingle with the clients, which is ample time for me to make further arrangements with my newly found lady friends.

The girls had driven down from Tampa for the weekend. They were at The Fontainebleau in North Miami Beach for another night and asked me if I would like to join them. It is a stunning hotel right on the beach that is featured in the movie Scarface. (It is the scene where Pacino's friend attempts to chat up a lady by the pool and ends up getting a slap for his trouble).

The girls left me at one of the many bars whilst they went to get cleaned-up. There were tables in candlelight by the pool area, so I got a drink and found myself a table when the girls reappeared in double sharp time. They are on the gear and made no secret of it.

"Do you like blow"?

"Of course,".

"Do you want a bump"?

I was confused.

"Do you call cocaine, blow"?

"Sure, what do you call it"?

"Any number of things but not blow"!

She lines me a nice big fat one, kisses me full on the lips and says, "Come on, we are going to South Beach".

I am absolutely flying now. We got dropped off at third and Ocean because it would give us a chance to look at what place we would like to go when I say.

"I wanna dance".

"So do we".

We are at the bottom of seventh and Ocean when I notice a happening little place about fifty yards up on the right.

Predominantly frequented by South Americans, we ordered some mojitos and shots of tequila. I was at the bar when I had a thought. If it is going to be like this for nine months, I am not going to survive. On the one hand, I will be a raging alcoholic, and on the other, I won't have a septum. Furthermore, I would be absolutely riddled, but I would worry about that another time, as my immediate future looked more than promising.

And so, it came to pass. They dropped me off in the morning and I limped to my shit hole of a cabin.

The Black Hole of Calcutta!

"You look like a fucking mess".

"Thanks, mate, you don't look so bad yourself"!

"Good night"?

"You could say that".

75

"Anyway, what do you think of the place"?

Whilst I was out working for England in an ambassadorial role, Alex had been the adult and cleaned the cabin. It was still tiny, but at least the smell was gone, and it was clean. More importantly, it was liveable.

I was assigned an empty blackjack table, which allowed me to have a good look at how the casino worked. The casino crew consisted of two cashiers, a manager, an assistant manager, a pit-boss, a Boxman, about fourteen dealers, and a slot tech. There was no need for supervisors as everybody was experienced. As we were at sea, there were no legal obligations to consider, no gaming act, no compliance, no eye in the sky, nothing. You played by our rules, or you didn't play at all. There were only two places you could play casino games legally in the States, Nevada and New Jersey, meaning that in 1986 most of our clientele had never seen the inside of a real casino. Which ultimately meant the players got ripped off on the odds they were paid. It was set-up with very small maximums giving the house an even bigger edge. There was very little roulette action as American's prefer craps and blackjack, and all the games are dealt at a much slower pace because we worked for tips. It was an absolute doddle. Throw in the fact we got a fat tip cheque every three months, and you could say the reservations surrounding my cabin were a distant memory.

El Casino Freeport (Princess) was my first experience of an American style gambling hall. It had fifty blackjacks, four roulette, and nine dice tables, with approximately five hundred slot machines. Most gaming staff were British, with a smattering of Bahamian dealers. The management were all Italian/American. When Fidel Castro overthrew Batista in 58, it ended the mob's casino association. Known as the jewel in the Caribbean, they had heavy investment in various hotels in Havana, and now that Castro was in power, it left a void in their casino empire, thereby needing to invest elsewhere of which Freeport was a recipient. It had a hotel next door to house high rollers, a golf course and a shopping mall. They leave nothing to chance in their pursuit of keeping you happy, so while you are dropping cash on the tables, you can rest assured your missus is being well looked after. It is a professional manufactured approach to ensuring you leave having done your bollocks, whilst looking forward to your next trip.

It was an eye-opener, as I was able to see first-hand how a casino was properly run. From the front door, the Americans are in a league of their own. It has always been an embarrassment to take part in how the casino game conducts its business in England. It is pathetic compared to our cousins across the Ocean. Is it any wonder that the business is on the wane here? The people in charge couldn't run a bath, because they are managed by bean counters rather than people that understand gamblers. *If you would like some consultation on how to run a casino, ask. Just saying!?!*

To my mate's surprise, I managed to locate him on a busy dice game.

"Alo son"!

"Ow are ya"?

"I'm on break in a minute".

"Sweet".

Two minutes later, we establish his day off is Wednesday, so I arrange for him to have a night out in Miami and return the day after. He was my sparring partner in London as we worked the dice table and various other activities, and more importantly, *he knew the rules.*

12

With the punters purring at the palm trees of the Caribbean, all I could hear was the Herbert screaming at the top of his voice, "I'll meet you in Pier One". My pal was in top form, so after we exchanged pleasantries, we got down to it.

"I know what you're thinking before it even comes out of your fucking mouth".

"What's the deal with the ship"?

"Don't know yet. It's my fourth trip, so I haven't had enough time".

"How much time do you need"?

"About three to four weeks".

"That's too long".

"It's new to us, out here!".

"I have done three trips on that boat".

"Really"?

"Yes, fucking really, and there is way too much heat on us boys that work on the Island".

"I'll bear that in mind!"

"It should be easy in Miami ".

"I need time to establish a routine".

"Get it sorted sharpish because I have a guy looking for someone like you".

"I don't want to meet him".

"He doesn't want to meet you either. He's only interested in the route and the readies"!

"Sweet".

"Anyway, take my box of fags, and tell me what you think".

I go to the toilet and find the biggest bag of cocaine I have ever seen in my life. With a nickel coin, I scoop a little bump and taste the goods.

"What do you think"?

"That's cream that"!

"It's untouched, straight out the aeroplane".

"How much"?

"A monkey ($500)".

It didn't take me long to do the math. Twenty-eight grammes in an ounce at eighty bucks a gramme is two thousand two hundred and forty dollars, but the beauty of this was in the purity. You could cut this three times, and it would still be considered good on the street.

"We'll do a dummy run today"!

"I was hoping you'd say that".

We ordered some conch, had a couple more beers and then it was time for a look at our new venture.

Without a flinch, I got back to my cabin, and deposited the yayo in a safe place. That was easy, but I needed a little time to develop a strategy. Like a child who is just about to start their six weeks summer holidays, I bound over to John's car in a state of euphoria.

The trip back to Miami was a blast, Ronnie gave me the night off. With beer a dollar a bottle and enough cocaine to feed Shepherd's Bush, we attacked the ship's entertainment venues with gusto. In the lounge bar played a band of typical American jazz followed by a show. The male singer had a more than adequate voice, and the three female dancers were very pleasant on the eye. After they finished, the team do a little walk around the lounge mixing with the clientele, but the moment they got to our table it was game over. The poor girls didn't stand a chance.

"Hi, guys"!

"What's appenin"?

"You guys from England"?

"London as it 'appens".

"You guys on vacation"?

"No, I work on board, and he lives in the Bahamas".

"What are you doing tonight"?

"Tobacco Road".

"Mind if we tag along"?

"Absolutely".

"It's a date"!

The girls carried on mingling. Cocaine was absolutely flooding Miami, with the vast majority coming through the Bahamas, so quite a lot of our clientele picked it up in Freeport. This was also my first experience of how crew members went through immigration. Subject to all sorts of demands, the crew were made to leave their bag on the floor, whilst being asked to walk approximately ten feet away so the dogs could do their thing, *not good*. It got a lot worse some sixty seconds in when one of the dogs took a more than passing interest in one of the bags. A bit of a kerfuffle ensued, finishing up with the owner of the bag identified, handcuffed and promptly marched off the ship. *Really not good!*

With my feeling of euphoria seriously on the wane, I went to my cabin to relax and give some thought to my recent experiences. The Bahamas was a doddle. However, Miami was a different kettle of fish. It would take a lot of planning, guile, and no little skill. Considering what I had just witnessed, I had my spirits lifted when I saw the girls at the gate. We got our passes and made our way over to Tugboat's.

After you pass the biggest reception desk in the world, turn left, about thirty yards in front of you is the entrance. On the right is a circular bar, on the left are tables and chairs, then a stage and a not so small dance floor. Tonight, a band was playing up-to-date covers, with the dancefloor absolutely hopping. I found John at the bar in deep conversation with Stud.

"Oi Oi".

"Alo son".

"Meet Stud".

"Hi Monz".

"You two know each other"?

"He's an old pal of mine".

"That's handy because he's our connection".

"It's in the stars, mate".

"You got my fags".?

"I have".

"I told you it was easy".

I ordered four Stud specials for John, myself and the two girls and decided to have a boogie. After John refuelled, we needed some time alone. We made our excuses to the girls, got a cab to the beach and found a little cabana on Washington and eighth. The modus operandi was simple, John would pick up in Freeport, I would get it on the ship, smuggle it into Miami and make the drop off to Stud at The Marriott. We had a deal at twenty-seven bucks a night with the hotel, so everyone that had a day off would find themselves a room for a couple of nights. It was big, but at first glance a little indiscreet. I was a little pensive. Initially, it looked easy, but as in all-new ventures, it is always best to do your homework.

That is why I needed at least two weeks. It would give me time to create relationships with the crew. Who worked what nights, who was more diligent in their approach to finding illegal contraband? I had been on the ship less than a week.

After a couple of mojitos, we decided to look at The Clevelander on Ocean Drive by way of a trip back to the hotel -

"A penny for your thoughts".

"I'm not sure about South Beach. It seems old".

"How much did you pay for the room"?

"Twenty-seven dollars".

"I have an idea".

"Go on".

"Rent an apartment".

"On South Beach".

"Why not"?

This got me thinking about the economics. It cost fifty-four dollars a week to spend a day off the ship at the hotel and about a hundred dollars a week to rent an apartment in Miami. It would not be in the most salubrious part of town, but it quickly became a no-brainer considering the privacy and sleeping issues.

"I'm off Monday next week, so I'll look into it".

"Don't look now, but the girls are here".

"Hi, guys".

"Hey, wanna drink"?

"Don't mind if we do".

And that was that! One of the girls says to John,

"Want to see my room"?

"See you in the morning".

Given these set of circumstances, the alcohol, cocaine, the sun rising on Miami, and a more than amorous dancer to contend with, you can almost forgive my state of mind. I had completely lost track of time, so when I was awoken by John looking like Marty Feldman on acid, I couldn't quite grasp what he was saying.

"It's half eleven".

"Bollocks".

"I'm working tonight".

"I was supposed to be working today".

"I'm sweet, I can get a flight about four. Only takes half hour".

"What the fuck am I gonna do"?

"No drama, son, you'll be sweet"!

I stood in the shower and brushed the previous evening's shenanigans out of my teeth. I had fucked up big time, but if the worst came to the worst, I would get a job with another cruise line.

"Morning".

In my haste to come up with an excuse, I had forgotten about the dancer.

"Ow are ya"?

"I love the way you guys talk".

"Get in the shower, girl. It's a beautiful day, so I thought we could spend a day at the beach"!

I called John and told him of my intentions.

"I can't, mate, my flights at three, so I'm going to spend my time here with the young lady".

"Sweet".

"I'll come and meet you at the ship. We'll do lunch at Pier One"!

"I look forward to it"!

I don't know whether it was the fact I had slept deeply, but I had a lot of energy. So, when lunch was over, I wanted to see what Miami had to offer.

We went east into the beach area. I was shocked at how run down and dilapidated it was. It was by no means a warzone, but it needed some investment. It was all there, the sun, the beach, the funky art-deco buildings. But it was in desperate need of someone who could attract new money.

We were minding our business walking down Washington when I saw a realtor (estate agency). I made an introduction and stated I was looking for a one-bed apartment. They had loads, so I arranged to come back on Monday to view and hopefully tie up another side of the plan.

"That's not a bad idea that"

"Getting an apartment"?

"Yes, the cabins onboard are pretty tight to say the least".
"Fancy a dip"?
"Let's"!
We spent the rest of the afternoon at the beach, had a couple of cocktails with dinner and an early night. It was perfect. The trip in the cab on the way to the port was a little uncomfortable as I was shitting myself. I was seriously concerned that my stupidity had cost me a good thing, so it came as no surprise as soon as I got in my cabin, Ronnie knocked on the door.
"I fucking told you"!
"Sorry, Ron"!
"You were seen at The Clevelander, then you were seen with two birds at Tugboat's".
"Guilty as charged!".
"I'm only kidding, son. Take it as your day off. Just be careful because if it happens too often, they keep you onboard until you get a transfer".
It was a bonus having Ronnie as my manager. He was not only a London boy but a Chelsea fan to boot. As long, as I played by the rules, he would have my back. We had begun to develop a relationship based on friendship as he took me under his wing, but we also got on because I never asked what he was up to.
"You are on the dice crew Monz".
"Cheers, Ron".
I watched every docking like a hawk. Who was in charge, who did what in terms of immigration? Where was the bosun, the quartermaster? Without a doubt, they were a lot tighter about security. There was a regimental feel about it, with a lot of dogs present as well. Everybody got searched. The scrutiny was intense. This had a completely different feel to it than midweek.
Monday morning, I was at the agency at nine o'clock on the dot, as I was eager to get business done. I don't know whether I was in a rush or liked what I saw, but I took the first place I viewed. With rent of four hundred and fifty dollars a month and a month's deposit upfront, I was in receipt to a furnished one-bedroom apartment at the back of Nineth and Ocean, approximately one hundred yards from the beach. *Sorted!*
A game of football was just what the doctor ordered, but it came with a warning. Be very careful with this mob as they don't

like us, and they play football somewhat differently. In other words (violently).

The game kicked off, and within a minute, we got a corner. As one of our side goes to take it, there are all sorts of shenanigans going on with the arm pulling, grabbing etc., when I got hold of one of them and put him on his arse. We were having none of it. If they wanted a fight, they could have one. If they wanted a game of football, they could have one of them too. We scored from the resulting corner leading to us giving them a proper hiding. However, to give them their due, they shook us all by the hand once the final whistle went. Especially a guy named Junior.

Inadvertently I made some new friends as it became clear that the boy from London not only liked his reggae music, but he could play football as well. Whenever the predominantly Jamaican boys got an opportunity to kick some ball, they would come to the casino and ask if I wanted to play. It was a real honour and proof that I had been accepted.

The flat was proving to be a real bonus as I could rest properly and privately at night, and more importantly, it gave me an opportunity to get a feel and flavour of Miami. The absolute number one rule here was not to draw attention to yourself. The casino crew didn't have a Danny I had an apartment. They never knew I had friends in the Bahamas. They thought I had a regular girl I stayed with most nights. I didn't tell them what I was doing, and they never asked. We were about a month in when I felt I had gained enough confidence in the layout. About two hours after we docked it was time to set the wheels in motion.

I made the meet in Freeport with John and went to see Stud to make the financial arrangements.

Miami was especially nice in the morning as I had developed a habit of going into the ocean for a swim. Get home, shower, get ready for work. It was about routine and consistency. I get to Freeport to be met by an excited John.

"Get in the car".

"I don't want to meet your guy"!

"You're not!".

On arrival, John pulls out the biggest bag of yayo I have ever seen in my life!

84

"What the fuck is that".

"A kilo".

"More like fifteen fucking years"!

"You would get the same if you got caught with an ounce or a kilo".

"Thanks for that".

"It's four grand your end".

"How much"?

"Four large, Stud will pay you tonight. He will give you eight. You take four. I get four. Now you can see why I was keen to get this started. I'm coming to Miami tomorrow, so you can give it to me then".

"How did you know I was off tomorrow"?

"It makes sense with you doing the run".

"Why are you coming to Miami".

"Because I have an account there, I can't bank that sort of money here as it would raise suspicion".

"Come to my apartment. We'll divvy up then".

"It's a date, good luck"!

He dropped me back, and I was afforded an easy passage back on the ship with my newfound status as one of the boys. However, I will never forget how heightened your senses become as you try to remain calm. The rush of adrenaline on that first trip is akin to an orgasm. You are sensitive to everything around you. On the face of it, you are cool, calm and collected, but underneath that facade, everything is going ten to the dozen. I was sweating like a convicted rapist, but that was OK as it was a particularly hot day. I went straight to my cabin to be met by Alex.

"You got a bird or something, Monz"?

"Yes, mate"

"Alright if I bring a bird back"?

"Fill your boots son"!

I was given last break to clear immigration. I had done the research, the right officers were in place, the gate crew were ready. One by one, you approach the desk to be met with the familiar line of,

"What's the purpose of your visit to the United States"?

'I'll get my washing done in the morning followed by some shopping for some toiletries etc., then I was hoping to get some time on the beach".

"Hope you enjoy it, have a good day. Before you go open your bag for me"!

"What"?

"Open your bag"!

I had placed my soiled smalls (which we enabled by smearing with a little shit), at the top along with my socks which turned out to be a good move as the smell that emanated from my holdall was so horrendous that it drew a little smirk from the officer,

"If I was you, I would get that washing done pronto".

I walk off the ship with my cocaine, get a cab to Tugboats, go through reservation at reception, call Stud and inform him that our new business venture was off and running. I had to be seen to do the same thing as everyone else, so I booked into the Marriott. Stud came to the room with the readies. We exchanged pleasantries and looked forward to working together!

13

South Beach Miami was a completely different animal in the mid-eighties than what you see today. It was in no way shape or form, the uber-trendy hot spot that it has become. The overall population were migrant workers from South America and Cuba who did the jobs Americans wouldn't do. Curiously, it also had a large older Jewish community lured there by a warm climate and cheap rent.

In 1986 the mega-popular TV show Miami Vice employed Gianni Versace as a consultant to elevate the two main characters, Crockett and Tubbs to worldwide fashion icons. He bought a house on the beach and opened a shop on Washington Avenue that was his best-performing outlet globally. Within a year or two, he brought along Madonna et al, modelling agencies started to spring up, police squads were increased and along with that came the boutiques, bars, clubs and restaurants. In a very short period, a TV show and a fashion designer had turned Miami from an area of ill repute into one of chic, vogue, and the place to be seen. And little ol' me was there to witness it.

My apartment was in the middle of the renaissance. It was ideally situated in terms of logistics because anything happening on South Beach was occurring right on my doorstep. It was literally history unfolding before my very eyes as, week by week, month by month, the cool and trendy of the US of A, wanted a piece of Miami.

Miami was growing on me big time. I had a great job, loads of readies, nice clobber, I had everything a man could want and need, but I also had the nous to be aware of keeping a lid on it. The overriding aspect in this charade I was living, was to be mindful that people are very much judged on what they wear and drive in the States, and I played the game to perfection.

I was about two months in now, and life was going well. We had created a little business venture that was pulling me in a very good living, I had a lifestyle that could be considered somewhat comfortable, I was known among the locals as a man that went to work, and I was a guy that tipped well in restaurants, bars and clubs etc. In fact, you could say I was living the dream when it happened. I was in a bar on the beach, minding my own business, when she walked in. South American, all six feet of her with corkscrew hair down to her waist, the body of a goddess, in other words, trouble with a capital T. I fell in lust instantly. I couldn't take my eyes off her, so rather than stand there dribbling, I got a seat outside. I was loving life when things were going to get a lot better,

"Hi".

"Alright".

"Would you mind if I sat here"?

"Be my guest".

"You're English".

"I am"!

"I am waiting for a friend of mine who is always late".

"Light Ale"?

"Sorry"?

"I'm having a mojito would you like one"?

"Sure, why not?".

"I'm David, by the way".

"Olivia".

Result! We must have sat there for ages talking all things Miami when ....

"What do you do"?

"I'm a croupier".

"A what".

"I work in a casino on a ship".

"Sounds like fun".

"It is".

As I was going to say something, she said, "Yes".

"I ain't said anything yet".

"I was hoping you were going to ask me out"?

"What you doing tomorrow evening?"

"Meeting you!".

"About eleven?"

"I look forward to it!"

I bounced all the way home.

There wasn't a soul on the beach as I went for my morning swim. It was run day, so I had to be bang on point. I did my breathing exercises and ten minutes of meditation in the morning sun, which was a little routine I learned from a hippie who lived just around the corner. He had done way too much LSD in the sixties, but he had some innovative ideas regarding the mind, which used correctly definitely paid off.

I ordered Cuban coffee with eggs at the pop up followed by a taxi. I arrive at our cabin and there's Alex hanging out the back of something for all his worth, "What's the time"?

"Nine o'clock" He didn't even break stroke.

"Bollocks, I'm off today"!

"Well, you better liven up son"!

With all sorts occurring, the familiar grunting and universal sexual language of, fuck me here, fuck me there, I squeeze into the shower room and get ready.

"You've got about ten minutes before we sail mate".

"Bollocks...shit...fuck!!!

It was one of the funniest things I have ever seen in my life, watching two adults attempting to get dressed and pack a small bag in an area the size of a shoebox. You would have thought we had just sounded the abandon ship alarm, but to be fair to them, they managed it...just.

The crew was small compared to today's standards. I knew everyone, so breakfast was a good way to discover what had gone on the previous evening. If anything, this ship was a fuck-fest with everyone banging each other. I didn't understand it as there were so many clients available daily, on the other hand, though, I did enjoy the wind-up as I would bellow across the room,

"Morning Bonnie, good night last night"?

To be met with stone-cold silence followed by a look that could kill. Clearly, she had gotten drunk and done something regrettable, but that was the 'Scandinavian Sun'.

We set sail, so I made my way to work when it became clear it was a busy day. This was good news as it meant the security resources of the ship would be concentrated on the passengers, and as it was midweek, immigration would be light in Miami too. As we opened, the clients flew through the door. All the seats on blackjack were taken, most of the colour on roulette was out, the dice table was busy on both ends, and the slots was doing good business. I was on the stick-on dice, going through my usual cockney routine. There was big bad red (Alex Rydzewski) the most insanely handsome six-foot-two lump from Blackpool, John Pang, a little Chinese/English ex-footballer that gave as good as he got and there was 'fingers', but more of that later. Ronnie had gone and in his place was a Chinese/Englishman named John Tang, a real casino guy and another proper gentleman. His problem was his inability to consume alcohol, which was highly amusing because he would do his champion-lagboat-impression after two bottles of becks.

We get to Freeport, and the ice cream that is John is beaming at me from the car park.

"Ow ar ya"?

"Sweet".

"You ready".

"I was born ready"!

We had synthesised our routine to a fine art. Once a week, he would pick me up from the ship, take me to a beach, followed by lunch at Pier One. It would never be the same day either, as again, we kept it fresh. So, I paid the bill and made my way to the crew gate. As per usual, the same boys were at the entrance alongside someone I had not seen before. This guy was Bahamian, and he was there to ensure things like bag searches were being carried out correctly.

Not good...

I normally exchanged pleasantries then made my way to the cabin, but not today. Marco was on, and he explained that, he felt it necessary to give my bag the once over. A towel, sunglasses, tropical suntan lotion and my board shorts were all the contents contained within. I get back to the cabin and take the kit off my body. The way we operated was always going to be a problem if this type of scenario presented itself, so after the first week, I thought it would be easier to cut the kilo into smaller pieces and tape it to my body. Although it was extremely risky, it worked.

I was on blackjack now, and it was much easier to converse with the passengers. On a busy dice game, you have your head down and your ass in the air, whereas on blackjack, you stand up straight and deal at your own pace. But you had a captive audience, and more importantly, we had the accent.

"Hey Monz, are you from London"?

"Yes, mate"!

"I know someone from London, John, do you know him"?

We don't know whether it was the motion of the ocean, the alcohol, or they may have just lost their minds. Still, it was a source of hilarity trying to explain to Americans that we had running water, electricity, we once had a great empire, and yes, there was more than one fucking John in London. Another thing that used to wind-me-up was trying to inform them of the game of cricket. And test cricket at that. For us, a draw is a draw, but, not in the States, you can have a tie. However, they will play overtime until a winner is declared. Can you imagine trying to explain to someone, that they often play for *five days,* and *no-one* wins?

It then came to light that the University of Miami American football team were onboard. I am by no shakes of the imagination considered small, but some of these guys are built like brick shithouses. They absolutely dwarfed me in terms of not only height but width as well, and I take my hat off to them.

I had a table full of them. We laughed, joked, and had a right giggle when I explained our swear words to them. A jerk, for example, is a (tosser or wanker). A fag, a (rear gunner), they loved it as they would use our terms. The crew in the pit were in a fit of giggles as these big men were going around calling out, wanker, tosser, are you a rear gunner?

I was particularly keen to disembark tonight as I had Stud to meet and Olivia from Bolivia. I went through my smuggling process of taping cocaine to my body. I was first in the queue and as I had no bag, I was straight off no drama. I got a taxi to my place to be met at the door by Stud. There was something different about him tonight, I couldn't put my finger on it, but it soon came to light.

"What the fuck is that"?

"A Rolex".

"What did we say? What the fuck did we agree on"?

"It's only a watch"!

"It's solid gold, you fucking idiot".

"That's a bit strong"!

"It's about ten grand on your wrist. Are you trying to get us nicked"?

91

"I'll get rid of it tomorrow"!

"Fucking right you will"!

I de-rigged the yayo, got the readies and informed Stud I had a date, and he was more than welcome to join us. I jump in the shower, change into some kit and float my way over to the Clevelander. She was outside.

I offered my hand by way of an English introduction. She leant in all South American by way of a kiss on the cheek, loaded with intent.

"You look good"!

"So do you"!

"Shall we"?

"Let's".

I am not one for PDA (Public Displays of Affection), but it made me extremely proud when she held my hand. We made our way to the bar, ordered a drink when Stud came bouncing over.

"Hey, Monz".

"Hey, Stud, meet Olivia".

"Hi, Olivia, would you guys like to join us".

"Absolutely"!

In the corner sat a blonde who happened to be on the arm of Stud. We made our introductions, and as luck would have it, the girls got on like a house on fire, leaving me to discuss what had gone on earlier. Rule-number-one do not draw any unwanted attention to yourself, and two, under no circumstances buy anything ostentatious.

"I suppose I'll have to get rid of the Corvette too"?

"Are you fucking kidding me"?

"I couldn't help myself"!

"John is here tomorrow, we'll discuss everything then"!

"Sweet. OK, see you tomorrow".

I suggested somewhere a little more intimate because I had an ulterior motive on my mind. We left the Clevelander and were making our way back to 8th and Ocean when I felt a tug on my hand as we arrived at the bottom of nineth, my street. She pulled me in a little closer, never said a word, just looked at me. It was raining, we got a little closer. Still nothing, then she said,

"Don't you live over there"?

I never responded. I stood there motionless, mesmerised by her beauty. We stood there looking at each other until we realised, we were getting soaked. I took her by the hand. Without saying a word, I led her into my apartment.

Olivia was my girlfriend now, and in an ever-increasingly beautiful people environment, *she was the head turner!* Everywhere we went, people would stare, unashamed, unabashed, in most cases downright ogle, but that's the price you pay for going out with women such as her. She was a dancer by trade, a contemporary dancer I hasten to add who went out with a guy that had nothing on the surface. She would occasionally ask me why we ate in the best of food establishments, but I would always brush it off with some excuse or another. I also made sure that I kept in shape and had plenty of dough, but fair play to her she never asked, and I never volunteered any information. We just enjoyed each other's company.

14

The alarm went at five am as I got up earlier on run days. I leant over a slightly stirred Olivia to switch it off, when she grabbed my arm and held it tight. "Morning"
"Morning baby"-
"Do you have to go?"
"I got to see a man about a dog"
"What"?
"It's a London fing"
"I don't understand?"
"You wouldn't. I'm going for a dip. Be back in arf our!"
I brushed me teeth, put me boardshorts and flipflops on and wrapped a towel around me neck. I flew down the stairs, got to the bottom of nineth and Ocean, crossed the road, when all-of-a-sudden it hit me. The horizon. The sun was coming out of its slumber, there was a tinge of red in the sky, the water sparkled, and the sand of South Beach Miami declared itself open for business. I sat on the wall that divides the pavement and the beach to give myself a few seconds to grasp the moment.

There wasn't a soul around apart from one guy that was sat staring at the sea. I gave myself some space to pass him enroute for me dip, when suddenly -
"Morning David"
"Sorry!"
"It's Junior. I'm a waiter on 'The Sun'"
"Please excuse me I didn't recognise you. You're up early!"
"I came to see you. I've been sat here for about an hour"
My heart started beating a little faster and my mind started to race.
"I wanted to talk to you about something"
"Go on!"
"You know David, there is a Captain, Chief Engineer, Staff Captain, Hotel Manager and a couple of other officers, but let me tell you something, I run the boat!"

"Don't you mean ship?"

We both laughed, which lightened the mood.

"Hugo looks after the Filipinos, and I the Jamaican's"

"And?"

"Do you want me to spell it out for you? There is not a thing that goes on that I don't know about. I've been waiting for someone like you. You do things quietly, discreetly. You have the right connections. The boys won't deal with us as someone fucked-up, so they shut the operation down!"

"What the fuck are you talking about?"

"See, that's what I like. You look as innocent as the day is long but we both know what I am talking about!"

"Go on!"

"I have a little black book that resembles a copy of War & Peace. I have an army bringing through eight balls, quarters, even half ounces, but it is taking too long to get to where I am trying to go"-

"What's the proposition?"

"I can guarantee, and I mean guarantee that it gets on in the Bahamas, and safely arrives in Miami. No drama or threat to you"

"Guarantee! that's a strong word!"

"Listen my friend, do you think we like working eighteen-hour days just so we can support our families that we don't see for months at a time. I want, sorry, would like to move things on a little quicker and you are the man to facilitate that"-

"So, I'm a facilitator now, am I?"

"Call yourself, whatever you want David, but I genuinely hope you can help me. Have a think about it? Just remember I can move as much as you want, whenever you want!

"Cost?"

"Thousand a key!"

"Leave it with me for a day or two. I'll speak to my people in the Bahamas"-

"I hope we can do business"-

"Fuck it. Meet me at Pier One at six just before the ship leaves for Miami"

"I was hoping you were going to say that"

"We'll try a load today and if that goes OK, we may be able to do something!"

We said our goodbyes and I threw my boardshorts and I into the Ocean. I got back to the apartment and Olivia making coffee.

"How was the water?"

"Sweet, but I've got to go, or I'll be late for work"-

With a smirk as wide as Harrods she starts climbing into bed, "You sure you have to go!?!

There was quite a game brewing on dice when I get tapped out by John the guvnor. "I need to have a word with you on the back deck!"

It's all happening today I thought. We open the doors to the deck and there is a band playing archetypal soft reggae music, the water is as smooth as a baby's bum and not a cloud in the sky. The pool was busy with lots of young talent on display enjoying a pina-colada, the bar was packed with seafarers looking forward to a day, doing whatever they fancied in the Bahamas, and there's me thinking 'I'm getting paid for this'. John started,

"I've been watching you, David!"

Here we go!?!

"Your dealing has come on leaps and bounds of late, how do you feel about promotion to Boxman?"

"To be fair, the game is a lot easier to deal here, I don't think I'm that good, but I suppose the money would be nice"-

"Good, that's settled then. I'll let head office know as they need someone on the 'The Sky' sharpish!"

"Hold on a minute. I'm moving ship?"

"You're going to Cape Canaveral"-

"Let's not be so hasty John. I get on with the crew, I love the run and more importantly, I just met a girl"-

"Fuck off Monza, you'll meet another one. Don't tell me you're in love?"

"No John, but I absolutely love Miami, plus I've made friends. I ain't been here that long mate, give it to someone else"

"Don't you want to think about it?"

"Thanks for the offer, but I'm one hundred per-cent positive!"

96

"OK son, but keep it in mind for future reference as they are thinking about you"

"Will do mate. Thank you!"

That was close. That would have been a right nause, as clearly, I couldn't discuss what I was really getting up to. It also got me thinking in terms of time frames. If I have only got a small window to make a lot of money, there was only one thing left to do.

John picked me up as per from the harbour to take me to his gaff, however, we stop at the International Bazaar when I broach the question,

"I might have found something"-

"Fucking knew it!"

"What does that mean?"

"It means, I fucking knew it!"

"Met some geezer on the ship"-

"And?"

"I'm going to try him today to see how it pans out"-

"How did you meet him?"

"We know each other from playing football together. He's the guvnor of all the Jamaicans. Works in the restaurant. Trust me, I've got a good feeling about this"-

"What do you mean, trust you?"

"He guarantees he can get it on and off no problem, but he has no means to work with the sort of connections we have. I like him!"

"You better know what you are fucking doing!"

"If it goes well today, which it will, there's something else to discuss"-

"You wanna go larger?"

"It makes sense"-

"We've got an absolute blinder, and you wanna fuck-it-up?"

"I want to nause it?"

"That's what I said!"

"I take all the risk. I tape the shit to my body for four large with the potential of getting a fifteen"

"When you put it like that"-

"There's very little risk with massive upside. It's a no brainer!?!"

"OK, it's your life, lets hit Xanadu, have a couple of lite-ales and take it from there"-

"Sweet!"

"Hold on a minute. How much?"

"A grand per key, plus a monkey for the cab driver"-

"Take that out of my end, you can do it next week"

"Fuck that, we go tomorrow"

We had a right giggle at Xanadu trying to kill each other with jet-skis. We brought some beer and during one of our duels I managed to swerve just in time for him to go flying in the air with his new Ray-Ban Clubmasters. I laughed myself stupid as he went berserk watching his new glasses sink to the bottom of the Ocean. The owners of the skis were over in seconds but as I explained the stupidity of spending $150 on a pair of sunglasses, they both laughed too. It's not like he needed the readies.

We go back to the flat and load up the motor with the contraband. John's very quiet, then "I'm not happy"

"Really? Which one of the seven dwarfs are you?"

"Very fucking funny!"

"I was alright on four large a week mate"-

"So was I, but the risk far outweighed the reward. We might as well get rich while we're at it. Makes perfect sense to me!"

"OK, have it your way, but if you get nicked, we don't know each other"-

"Hundred per cent!"

We pull into the port area, and I indicate for Junior to join us.

"You, OK?"

"All good!"

"This is my business partner John, you have never met him and if you are ever asked, you have never seen him before either"-

"I know the rules"-

"The parcel is wrapped in a towel in a beach bag, in the boot. At precisely midnight tonight you'll take the package through the taxi rank at pier 6 and into the carpark directly across the road. There will be a yellow Miami cab with this number plate waiting for you. Get in the back, make small talk and leave. That's your end taken care of. Short, sharp, sweet!"

"That's it?"

"That's it!"

"What about the dough?"

"I'll sort you in the morning. I'll come to the restaurant, give you the nod, then come to my cabin"-

With a smile as wide as Jamaica itself, Junior picks up the yayo and walks on 'The Sun' like a ghost. I look at John, he looks at me. "Well, that was sweet"

"See you tomorrow"

"Be ready tomorrow"

"Don't you want to wait and see what occurs first?"

"Do I fuck! I've got a feeling in me bones"-

The dice table was kicking right off. There were bets coming in left right and centre as it was silly busy for a Tuesday. In fact, the whole casino was at it, and I was buzzing like a Bee. "Inside-outside, do or don't come, lay or take the eight" The atmosphere was incredible, so-much-so that it came as a bit of a disappointment when the guvnor called last shooter. I had completely forgotten about the other thing as this is what really floated my boat, (if you'll excuse the pun).

We disembark no drama. I get into the cab and instruct my driver to take me home. "You OK boss?"

"Couldn't be better"

I met this guy on the dice table on 'The Sun' on one of our cruises. We struck up a friendship by virtue of my accent. He was from South America somewhere and was fascinated by my English pronounciation. It was as if he was starstruck or something, but I kept bumping into him in the strangest of places, including him waiting for me every night. We pull up outside my apartment block and I get in the front seat.

We shook hands. "What are you doing tonight?"

"Working"-

"How would you like to do a job for me?"

"Depends?"

"I need you to go to the port of Miami at midnight. A black guy is going to get in the back. He will leave after about five minutes, but he will have left a beach bag under the seat. Do you think you could deliver that bag to me straight after?"

"That's it?"

"That's it. You get that to me safely and I will give you five hundred dollars"-

"No problem, I'll see you later"-

I get into the apartment and run the shower; it was a hot night. I'm flicking through the million TV channels when the door goes. "Who is it?"

"Jorge!"

It was half twelve. "Come in"

He had the beach bag.

"I lost track of time"-

"This what you wanted?"

"Exactly that!"

I gave him the readies.

"Do you want to work for me Jorge?"

"Fuck, yeah!"

"How much do you make in a week?"

"Not as much as this" pointing at the money I just gave him.

"Good, don't pick me up tomorrow as it will look suspicious. Be around the same place at the same time. Junior will deliver to you, then you to me"-

"Thank you, David,".-

"Don't thank me, Jorge. Just make sure you get my parcel to me"-

"I can do that"-

"Sweet, see you tomorrow"-

Stud showed up at one. "Don't take this the wrong way, but you are good at this. You should think about.............."

"Already at hand. Be here tomorrow, same time"-

"I fucking knew you was the guy!"

He counted the eight large and left with a spring in his step.

"Before you go Stud, bring sixteen grand tomorrow"

"You the man David, you the man"-

I fell into a sleep of coma proportions as my alarm clock woke me at seven, with Olivia beside me.

"How the fuck?"

"The door was open"

In all the excitement of last night, I had taken my foot off the pedal. I was raging at my own stupidity, but I couldn't let Olivia see it. "Are you working today?"

100

"I am"-

"Say hello to the Bahamas for me"-

"Of course,"-

"Are you back at the normal time?"

"I have to go to Lauderdale tonight, I'm not sure what time I'll be back" I shouted from the shower.

"Ah that's a shame"-

I walk into the bedroom, and she is lying there in just a pair of Alan's. All the blood drained from my body into my cock. If I had turned round sharpish, I would have knocked a fucking wall down. "I was beginning to think you didn't like me?"

"I've got to go baby. If I don't go to Lauderdale, I'll be in the Clevelander about oneish. I fancy a couple of lemonades tonight as I'm off tomorrow"- Her eyes lit up.

"Hopefully see you at one, have a good trip!"

What a sight for sore eyes she was, but there was work to be done and people were depending on me. I felt like I was building something.

As it was a Wednesday the ship sailed with few passengers, so I was stuck on a dead BJ table minding my own business, when the guvnor comes over. "Shut that table Monz. Take the rest of the shift off as I'm not going to open the dice table until this evening"-

I go down a deck and into the restaurant to find Junior.

"I'm off until tonight, so pop down anytime you like"- Within fifteen minutes there's a knock at the door.

"Come in Junior"

I gave him the readies in crisp one-hundred-dollar bills. "Now that's what I'm talking about!"

"Looks good so far!"

"Let me know when you want to go again"-

"Today. Be at the same place, same time"

"You don't fuck about"-

"This is the last time we meet at that place as it is not appropriate, but I didn't have enough time to make alternative arrangements"-

"Relax David, everything's cool!"

"Just be there!"

With a firm handshake and a knowing wink, he departed, leaving me to sort out the business.

We get to Freeport where John is waiting for me in his car.

"How'd it go?"

"Double sweet. Now let's get out of here, I want to meet your guy"-

"He wants to meet you too"

Roughly half an hour later we arrive at our destination and are ushered inside a typical Bahamian residence.

"I'm Floyd, you must be David, or do I call you Monza?"

"Let's keep it David for business purposes"-

"I like that. OK David, what's the move?"

"I want to increase the loads"-

"By how much and when?"

"I'd like to do two key a day, three times a week"

He sat in his chair, raised his hand to his face, which by now had a deep frown on his forehead, stared at me for about two minutes, then,

"That's a leap of faith. Do you have any idea who I work for?"

"Do I need to know?"

He laughed, then a great big smile came over him.

"You've got some balls; I'll give you that!"

"Not really. I have a little operation that requires co-operation in the right places. So long as you grease the right palms and pay your people on time, it's not difficult"

The reality of it was that I had done one successful run with my new guys, Junior and Jorge. Keeping the team small and tight was my MO moving forward, so I pressed on.

"How about we do two key today?"

"Think you can handle it?"

"There's only one way to find out!"

Floyd stood up, went over to the back door and called out a name I didn't catch. Twenty minutes later the guy returns with the yayo.

"There's your two key David"-

"Good doing business with you"-

"Don't count your chickens just yet. If you get it to Miami, I'll be impressed!"

With the contraband in the boot, John and I drove to Pier One for lunch and a drink. I needed one. John spoke first, "What have we got ourselves into?"

"A good little number. You should know, you made the introductions"

"A key a week was fine, but this is something else"-

"For fucks sake, grow up!"-

"It might be alright for you Monz, but I'm getting scared"-

"Of what? With the greatest respect you do fuck-all. Without you we wouldn't have this. But we have, so let's just fucking get on with it!"

"You're off tomorrow, I'm coming to Miami for further talks"-

"Don't waste your time mate, I'm done talking and anyway, I haven't seen Olivia for more than a week"-

"All fucking day?"

"Have you seen my girlfriend?"

"She's a good bit of kit is Olivia, I'll give you that, but it's not me I'm worried about, it's you!"-

"Don't give me that bollocks, I'm a big boy, I can look after meself!"

I had completely lost track of time. It was seeing Junior across the road trying to remain inconspicuous, that I realised we were late. We paid the bill, darted across the road and nigh on bumped him into the car. "It's the same coup, only this time there is two key"-

"No problem, David"-

"I'm off tomorrow so I'll sort you out Friday"

"As I said, no problem"-

Bang on 12:30am Jorge raps my door. He enters, walks into the bedroom, drops the bag and I give him the readies.

"There's a thousand bucks here!"

"You get five hundred a key. That way I can rely on you to maintain your professionalism, integrity and most of all your discretion. This is strictly business from now on. Don't get lairy, lagboat, and especially 'don't get high on your own supply'!"

"Thank you, David"-

"As I have said before, you don't have to thank me, just do the fucking job! We go again Friday. Same place, same time"

Stud turned up about fifteen minutes later. "You're like a team of seasoned professionals"-

"Look Stud. The only way this works is by keeping a low-profile. So, for future reference, our social relationship is out the window. It is nothing personal. It is what it is!"

"How do you keep a low-profile with Olivia?"

"You let me worry about that"-

I jumped in the shower, put some kit on and literally ran round the corner to The Clevelander to meet Olivia. I couldn't wait to see her. As I enter, she stood up from her bar stool, walks over and kisses me full-on-the-lips! "Hi baby"-

"Alo girl"-

"Wanna drink?"

"Yes, I do!"

It was the start of two of the best nights of my life. We didn't stay long as I suggested somewhere a little more intimate. We spent the next twenty-four hours completely ensconced in each other. We drank a little, danced a little, had breakfast, went to the beach, had lunch, went back to the beach, had dinner, went to a club, and somewhere in amongst all of that, we made a lot of love.

At some point early Friday morning, the sun peering through the window, stirred me. I was bang in trouble. Not from my little business, but Olivia. Her whole being had enveloped me, she had me hook, line and sinker. I wriggled out of her embrace, brushed my teeth, put my shorts and flipflops on and crept out the door.

This was my favourite time of the day. I swam for about ten minutes, then parked myself on the beach. I closed my eyes and went into deep critical thinking mode.

I had created a little business venture that carried enormous risk, so with this in mind, I came up with something that virtually put that to bed. It was my participation that had to be taken out of the equation, so it was time to see Floyd with my new strategy.

I had a spot of lunch in the ship restaurant as I wanted to see Junior for payment purposes. Freshly sorted as soon as we get to Freeport, I jump in a taxi to see John, and inform him that the business has reached expansion stage. I also informed him I was off on Monday, and it was a good idea for him to come to Miami as I had twenty grand of his in my little safe. That put a smile on his face.

"Olivia is in New York performing for a week so we can have a day together"-

"Sweet, I'll book it off now. If I don't see you over the weekend, I'll see you at your place Monday. I'll get an early flight"-

I had a meet with Floyd at a bar in the International Bazaar to formulate a strategy. As I walk in, he stands up, holds his hand out by way of a greeting and offers me a drink.

"I'll have a lager beer please"-

"Make that two!"

"I have to say David, I know a lot of people in this business, jerks, assholes, wanna be gangsters, real fucking gangsters. But you, you're different"-

"I'll tell you what you like about me. I go about my business efficiently, professionally. I have no desire to draw attention to myself"

"Exactly. So, what's the plan?"

"The MO is two key a day three times a week, Monday through Friday"-

"Too much heat at the weekend?"

"Way too many 'old bill,' creeping about! There's also something else I would like to discuss"

"Go on"-

"I need your number to let you know what days we go. I also want to stop collecting it myself. Do you have the means to get it to the port without me collecting it personally?"

He laughed out loud at that question.

"I take it that's a yes"-

"You can rest assured my friend, that it's a yes"

"How would you like to proceed?"

"Bring him to me, I want to meet him personally"

"Are we ready to go today?"

"Do you see that guy sat in the corner. That's Charles, he works for me. He's going to drop you at the port"-

"Sweet. I'll introduce him to Junior, then that's my end in the Bahamas over"-

"Even better"-

I called the barman over to pay the bill and open a bottle of Dom Perignon and put it on ice for Floyd, A nice touch I thought. We shook hands and made a meet to see each other next Friday to catch up. Floyd looks at Charles and nods his head to the side to indicate we are leaving.

On approach to the port, I see junior and tell him to meet us outside Pier One. After basic introductions I inform the pair, they are our team in Freeport. I also furnish them with the news that next week we go Monday, Tuesday and Thursday.

15

The casino was busy all the time as it was in the middle of summer. Dice game after dice game, cards in the air, roulette balls spinning, Miami to the Bahamas and back. I could think of worst places to be. The renaissance had begun. Little trendy cafés and bars started to appear. Cars were bigger, more expensive. The rich and famous were starting to come to Miami in their droves. Olivia and I were part of the furniture now, as we were always invited to the best parties, and because a lot of modelling agencies pitched up, there were beautiful people everywhere.

However, I had a first world problem that needed sorting lively. As a result of my successful career in the cocaine world, I couldn't get all the readies in the little safe in my apartment so I would have to move it to Tampa, where a pal of mine lived. He was connected to our line of work and had a five bed, four bath, swimming pool, tennis court and about five acres, detached house. We agreed that I could stash it in his safe until I had found a system to wash my money. It was only two hundred grand, but there wasn't a bank that would accept that kind of deposit in readies anywhere in Florida, not without raising suspicion anyway. It was my fault as I hadn't given it any thought. I was making the best part of thirty large a week but because it was coming in thick and fast, I got Blaise about the whole affair.

I decided to hire a car and inform Olivia we were going on a road trip. I had two days off so with said car and an excited Olivia in the front, I loaded an overnight bag and the readies in the boot. As it was a four-hour drive, we agreed that we would drive straight there, book into a hotel, go to the beach and find somewhere nice for lunch. Lovely!

We were about an hour in, going north on the 75, through the Everglades and Alligator Alley, when an unmarked police car with flashing blue lights pulls aggressively alongside. With both of us doing about eighty the guy in the passenger seat pulls his shooter pointing it at Olivia,

"Pull over, pull the fucking car over!" he screamed.

That's a bit much for speeding I thought. So, I stop at the side of the road, when the two of them get out of their car with their guns cocked.

"Hands on the wheel, hands where I can fucking see 'em man!"

I Put my hands on the wheel, with Olivia putting hers on the dash. She looked at me with genuine fear in her eyes, but I knew what this was, I was getting turned over. Holding his badge up and with a gun about two inches from my face, he says "Pop the truck"

"What?"

"Pop the fucking trunk!"

"What d'you mean?"

He pushes the gun into my face. At the same time Olivia starts screaming, "The boot David, the boot" He pushes the gun so hard into my face my nose is bending.

"Do you mean open the boot?"

"Yeah man, pop the fucking trunk!"

With the boot open, his colleague goes in search of my money. Seconds later with the bag in their possession, they walk to their car without so much as a backward glance.

"What the fuck was that, and why did they take your bag?"

"I've just been turned over"-

"What does that mean?"

"It means I've just been robbed!"

"Of what? Your beachwear? Your taste in clothes is not that good!"

"No Olivia, about two hundred grand!"

She tightened up, went quiet and let out a little gasp.

"Do you come from money or something David?"

"Do you think I'd be working on the SeaEscape (The Scandinavian Sun) if I did?"

"I dunno, you seem to have a nice little life to me!"

"Not two hundred fucking grands worth it ain't!"

That was the end of that conversation as not only was I getting angry, but Olivia had gone into shock. She was crying uncontrollably, tears streaming down her face and rather weirdly she kept apologising. "What are you apologising for?"

"There was no need to stick his gun in your face!"

I sat silently for about five minutes while I let the rage subside,

"Fuck them cunts! They ain't gonna ruin my weekend"

I looked at Olivia to analyse her state of being. She seemed a lot calmer. Then she mouthed the words, "I love you!"

"What?"

"I thought he was going to shoot you!"

"Don't be silly, they're not going to shoot me on the 75 in broad daylight"

"They did a good impression!"

"There's nothing I can do now, but I'm due in the Bahamas in two days so I'll get the ball rolling then"-

"As long as you are OK baby!"

"I've still got chunks of readies on me. Fancy Tampa?"

"Fuck yeah!"

"Let's go!"

I didn't bother calling my mate as my mind was all over the place. The readies didn't bother me either as I could get that back in no time. It was the fact Olivia had mentioned those three words, eight letters and one meaning.

In the midst, of having a drink at some swanky bar on the waterfront, I asked a waiter if they had a phone. I called Floyd to give him the news,

"This is not good!"

"You're telling me!"

"Don't say another word on the phone, when are you next over?"

"Tuesday"-

"Meet me in Pier One. I'll be waiting for you"

"OK See you then"

We tried to have a blast in Tampa, but if the truth be told my head wasn't right. I couldn't get Junior, Jorge or Stud out of my mind. One of these fucking Herbert's had gotten greedy. I was alright one minute and livid the next. The reason I always paid the full amount owed and promptly was to keep this sort of thing from happening. Junior was getting six large a week, Jorge three and Stud was working for Floyd and he was doing alright for himself. Where did this come from?

As we pull into Freeport, Floyd was waving at me. You could see from half a mile away he looked concerned. So, as soon as I get to the restaurant we get to it, "What the fuck happened?"

"I got robbed is what happened"-

"Explain in minute a detail as you can"-

I gave him the blow-by-blow account. The gun in my face, the badges we couldn't see, to knowing where to look for the money.

"Who knew you were moving the money?"

"No one"-

"Are you sure?"

"Hundred percent"

"How many in the team?"

"Junior, Jorge and Stud?"

"Did any of them know?"

"Only Stud knows about the safe!"

"David, I have a lot of money invested in you. It's part of my job to protect you!"

"What do you mean invested in you?"

"I mean I do very well out of the product you are moving for us"

"Am I gonna get my two hundred large back?"

"No, but we'll make it up to you! I have a few ideas of how to flush them out. Did your mate in Tampa know?"

"Yes, he did but he wouldn't have done it as two hundred grand to him is like a tenner to me"-

"Did they follow you from Miami?"

"I don't know, I don't think so!"

"So, they knew the plate? Who else knew you were in that car?"

"Olivia and me!"

He raised his eyebrows and had a deep frown on his forehead.

"Where and how did you meet Jorge?"

"On a cruise, on 'The Sun"-

"Explain!"

"We had a busy dice game. I was on the stick going through my normal routine and he was playing"-

"Did he know how to play?"

"What do you mean?"

110

"Did he know what he was doing?"

"Where the fuck is this going?"

"I'm trying to establish how this relationship started!"

"Yes, he had a pass line bet with odds and a bet on the six and eight. Archetypal American action!"

"Anything suspicious?"

"Nothing that's obvious"

"We'll have to come back to it, because it's definitely not Junior, and Stud works for us!"

"How do you know it's not Junior?"

"We had him checked"-

"And me?"

"It's you that's the mystery!"-

"Very fucking funny"

"Here's what we are going to do"

"At fucking last!"

"Nothing!"

"What"

"I mean nothing, nada, you don't mention it. Play it out as if nothing has happened"

"How the fuck are we going to find out who chored me readies?"

"Whoever it is will be different. You won't notice it at first but trust me on this – 'a rat, is a rat'.

I was angry at first, but then it made sense. Floyd was an old campaigner, a wise old head who clearly knew what he was doing so I let it play.

Jorge arrived at my place dead on 12:30am as per, Stud about fifteen minutes later, in fact to be brutally honest, if they were in on it, their acting skills were De Niro/Pacinoesque. There was no point worrying because I worked for the right people, so I was protected. I was what was known as a good earner and for their end, no-one could get pinched, but they made chunks of readies. So, I went to work.

16

With most of the crew being Jamaican, there was a buzz around the day. The preparation had been going on for a few days with the captain agreeing to pay for the food that consisted of copious amounts of curried goat, oxtail and dumplings, ackee and codfish, jerk chicken, coconut rice and peas, in fact, everything Jamaican. Throw in the fact they love a stout, and I was winning.

I was off for a couple of days, but there was no way that I was going to miss this party. As soon as the ship docked, Olivia and I were at the port and went straight to the back deck to enjoy the festivities.

Olivia and I threw ourselves at the party with gusto. We ate, danced, drank, we were having the time of our lives when I noticed my mate *(finger's)* getting involved in something that I thought he might like to know a little more about.

He was in deep conversation with an extremely attractive American purser who had clearly drank too much. He had this cheeky grin on his face as I know he liked this young lady. He had his arm around her. She was snuggling into him. If you had not have known them, you could be excused for thinking they were a couple. However, I was frantically trying to get his attention, and he was trying his hardest to ignore me. It was a real game of cat and mouse as I leant in to ask him if I could have a word, with him giving me the cold shoulder. It went on for ages, with the pair of them getting drunker by the minute, so I confided in Olivia.

She gasped, "You have to tell him".

"I know".

"But look at him"!

He looked as happy as a pig in shit. His grin was even bigger, but his eyes were glazed over, so I got hold of him by his arm.

"There's something you should know".

"Jog-on Monz"!

"I need to tell you something"!

"I won't tell you again, fuck-off"!

I honestly tried to be a mate, but I had reached the point of no return. Fuck him, I'll let him get on with it. I grabbed hold of Olivia by the arm,

"Where are we going"?

"Downstairs".

"Let's wait till we get back to yours".

"It's not about us".

"Oh my God, have you told him"?

"I tried".

Olivia started to giggle because he was having none of it. We watched as they entered his cabin. It won't be long, as all the foreplay had been done upstairs. We could hear her trying to stop him. There was a few seconds silence, then the sound of feet stomping, the door opened, before the sight of *(finger's)* standing their stark bollock naked, as limp as a dead rabbit.

"You could have told me"!

"I tried".

"Try fucking harder next time"!

And with that, he produced her prosthetic leg.

He wrenched it orf in the heat of battle. He held it up, handed it to me, done an about-turn, went back from whence he came, and just bloody well got on with it. What a man, what a legend!

It was still only early, so I suggested a nightcap at Tugboats as I hadn't been there in ages, and to kill two birds with one stone, it would be good to see Stud. I had a meeting with him and John the next day, but I thought we could have a couple of Stud specials to finish off the evening. So, imagine my surprise when I learned he quit a month ago. This was news to me, but I am sure there was a perfectly good reason for it.

Olivia had drawn me into a relationship I didn't want to be involved in. I was vulnerable because I was starting to develop feelings for her, which would have to be carefully managed because I knew deep down that I may have to chip at a minute's notice.

17

The following day John, Stud and I diarised a meeting for lunch on Ocean Drive to discuss our little project. John had flown in from the Bahamas early, so it gave me an opportunity to inform him of my concern's.

"How did you meet Stud"?

"In Tugboats, like you"!

"Something is not right".

"What do you mean"?

"He has given up his job, and a stranger answered his phone when I tried to call him".

"What"?

"I have a horrible feeling about this".

"I haven't seen him for a while, so we'll find out today what the crack is"?

"You mark my words J. He's up to summink"!

Two minutes later, a gleaming red corvette pulls up outside the beachfront cafe and out comes Stud and his solid gold Rolex. It was an entrance to create a stir and an exercise in how not to use discretion. I was going bananas. Before I could say anything, John jumped up, got hold of him and led him to the beach. It got even worst as they were involved in an altercation that was creating a scene. However, after about five minutes, it calmed down as John was getting through to him. They walked into the cafe, ordered lunch, and now we got down to business. Stud started.

"They want to meet".

"What? Who"?

"The people I work for"!

"You work for us, Stud"!

"No, Monz, I don't".

"We don't give a fuck who you work with"!

"These are not the sort of people you mess around with"!

"I couldn't give two fucks"!

"Well, these people do. All they want is a meet".

"Don't you get it Stud, this works because we keep it very low key, well we used to anyway"!

"What does that mean"?

"We, said at the beginning, don't get anything lairy. Remain inconspicuous"!

"I suppose Olivia is inconspicuous"!

"Leave Olivia out of this".

"You started it"!

Right there and then I knew this was the beginning of the end. There was something about Stud I didn't like. He had an arrogance about him, but because the *gentlemen* he wanted us to meet were now at the entrance, I would have given him a dig.

These *gentlemen* were clearly members of organised crime. They were as subtle as a hammer, with all six of them looking like something out of a movie. Introductions were made, so we got down to business as soon as pleasantries were exchanged.

"You're pulling six key a week out of the Bahamas".

I didn't answer because I knew where this was going.

"You have a good little business here; we think it's time to expand"!

"Explain expand".

"We're losing our influence on the Island. An English firm has taken over the casino, they're making it difficult for us. We need you to do one last job for us!"

"This little business of ours, work's for precisely the opposite reason that you are trying to get us nicked for"!

In the blink of an eye, I developed an exit strategy. We were in way over our heads, so I decided to play for time.

"Doesn't seem like such a bad idea"!

John looked at me aghast. You could see in his eyes he knew it was over, and there was only one way to play this.

"I'm going to need a couple of weeks".

"Why"?

"To sort out the gear".

"Who do you think supplies you. Do you think you are the only one's involved in this operation"?

I hadn't given this any thought as things were going so well. I looked at John, who just shrugged his shoulders. I looked at Stud, who was by now sat with his shoulders slumped. To make matters worse, they were trying to cut the deal in half, but I was having none of it. They needed me more than I needed them, and they knew it.

As soon as they left, it was as if we had taken a vow of silence. Neither Stud, John, nor myself said a word for ages, until I muttered the immortal.

"It's over".

"Fucking right it is".

We knew it was an exercise in futility to try and re-negotiate terms. We were kids involved in a man's game that had caught up with us. I was due to meet Olivia shortly, so I made excuses and left the two boys at it.

"How long you in town for"?

"Till tomorrow".

"I'll meet you here about nine if you fancy it".

"Sweet, see you then".

I didn't ask Stud, as I was so disgusted with him. Fundamentally it wasn't his fault, but I needed to vent my frustration on someone, and poor old Stud just happened to be in the firing line.

"What about me, Monz".

"I need to discuss a few things with John"!

"OK"!

"I'll see you at the weekend"!

I went straight to my apartment and called the office. As luck would have it, my mate was in, so I just laid it on the line.

"Alo mate. I'm burning the candle at both ends. Any chance I can get on a cruise for the last couple of months of my contract"?

"We have you in mind for something. The Canada Star out of New York. They have asked for a dice table, so I need to put a team on there. It's a fantastic itinerary. It's doing two one-week cruises to Bermuda, then a twenty-one-day repositioning cruise that takes in the East Coast, large parts of the Caribbean, up through the Panama Canal and into Los Angeles then back to New Orleans, which will be its home port. Then it's seven-day cruises to Key West, Playa Del Carmen and an overnight in Cozumel. It's a dream gig".

"Sounds good, when"?

"Two weeks"!

"Even better. Can I diarise that"?

"One hundred per cent"!

Two weeks was ideal as it gave me the time to get everything done. I had a healthy bank account, I could easily swerve the smuggling business, I also needed to get rid of the apartment, but all things considered, my only loss, was the deposit of four hundred and fifty bucks. However, considering my newfound wealth, this wasn't a problem. Olivia was the issue. She wasn't going to take this well, neither was I, but somewhere deep-down, I knew this day was coming.

I met John at nine at the Clevelander on the beach. There was a slight air of awkwardness as we knew this would not last forever. We had a good time. We made some money, and I had a wealth of experience to boot. With Olivia working, John and I threw ourselves at the Miami nightlife as if it was the last time, we would get to experience it. We hailed a cab for Tobacco Road, got about halfway there and then it started. I had never experienced rain or wind like this before. What the fuck was going on?

18

As it was my day off, I was unaware of the Storm Warning. The Scan Sun had booked all the rooms at The Marriott because when a hurricane or storm as this was coming, you take ships out to sea as they are considered dangerous, because of the potential damage. So instead of Tobacco Road, I told the driver to turn around and take us to Tugboat Annie's as I don't care how strong a storm is. *It won't knock down a hotel.*

By the time we got to Tugboat's, the gaff was absolutely packed with crew, having the time of their lives. This would be the worst storm in nearly three hundred years, so the opportunity to party as a group was uncommon. And boy, did they make up for it. John and I were champion-lagboat by now, having a great time when I made one of the stupidest mistakes of my life. Blame it on the beer, blame it on the gear, but an attractive Swedish purser was giving me the right once over, and silly bollocks fell for it. Don't get me wrong, I didn't have to get involved, but I couldn't help myself. We were all over each other when I suggested.

"Do you have a room"?

"Yes"!

"Let's go"!

Her mate was in the room, and as all the hotels were packed with crew from various liner's, we decided to go back to the ship. The trip in the car over was a blast as it was being shunted all over the road, and to be fair, we were both half-a-light, *not good!* So, we made our excuses and tried to get a taxi back to the hotel. We had to get off the ship as it was going out to sea with a skeleton crew because of the storm, so my Swedish friend set her alarm for half an hour as we were both falling asleep.

I was awoken by the light shining through the porthole. Much more of a concern, however, was the motion of the ocean. The Scandinavian Sun was an ocean-going liner, unlike most cruise ships that are built specifically for the Caribbean. However, the water levels exceeded the head purser's porthole, meaning we were rocking like fuck. The captain being the good man he was, managed to manoeuvre the ship into the eye of the storm, meaning it was calm. It was going to be a problem however, when it was time to exit the eye as this is where the storm is at its worst. There were very few provisions on the ship as nigh on everything had been taken off, so with that in mind, my newfound friend and I went on the hunt for something to eat.

As we scaled the stairs, it suddenly dawned on me that this was not a game or a fairground ride. No, this was dangerous. It killed twenty-two people in England, and there's me in the middle of it. But do you know something? I thought it was exciting. If you have never been on a cruise ship in a storm, you won't know what I am talking about, but I found it exhilarating to feel the power of nature beneath my feet. Ships are so vast these days you wouldn't know you were at sea, but in my day, ships were only five decks high, and you could feel the movement.

We were at sea for roughly three days when we limped into Bermuda. The turnaround was immediate too, as the skipper wanted to get back to Miami sharpish, so re-fuelled and restocked, we set sail with the wind at our backs, literally. When we arrived in Miami, the entire crew were waiting for us. The casino lot thought it was hilarious that I managed to get stuck on the boat. Anyway, in my ultimate wisdom, I played the 'I should not have been on the ship' card so well, that I managed to wrangle four days off, which was enough time for me to tie up my loose ends.

In the cab on the way over from the port, I started getting nervous, not because I was excited but in an agitated way. My gut was telling me that something was wrong. When I pulled up outside my apartment, the door was ajar. With tentative fingers, I pushed the door a little -

Olivia was tied to a chair with a look of sheer horror on her face, with two of the Italians casually sat next to her. One of them spoke. "Where the fuck have you been"?

"Bermuda".

"What the fuck were you doing in Bermuda"?

"I was in the middle of the storm"!

"We were waiting for you in the Bahamas".

"Well, then, you know we never went and anyway, what the fuck are you doing with my girlfriend"?

"She's the rat!"

Before I had a chance to answer, the boss walked in.

"Sit the fuck down",

"Donnie, Gio, take the girl for a ride".

Olivia couldn't look at me.

The boss (Tony) gave me the eyes.

"Did you know?"

"Know what?"

"She ratted you out!"

"No. It can't be true"-

"She's the informer. She's the one who passed information to the bent cops!"

I was staring at him not wanting to believe a word.

"You're a smart kid, work it out. Who else knew you were in that car, how they knew the plate? Anyway, Stud told us!"

"She wouldn't do that!"

"Don't be so fucking naïve son, she's even emptied your safe. So, before you leave, you are going to do one last thing for me".

This wasn't unreasonable.

"Johns fucked off, so Gio will pick you up from the ship tomorrow".

"What do you mean"?

"After our last meet, he went straight to work and resigned, left the island the next day. You are going to do this last thing for me, and then you can fuck off back to wherever you fucking come from"!

Donnie and Gio alongside a petrified Olivia come back in the room. I check my safe to see if Tony is telling the truth.

"Take her fucking gag off"-

She was crying, shaking.

"You fucking used me. That slaggy faced, muggy cunt put a gun in my face!"

She couldn't look at me. I told Donnie to take the ties off.

"Do you even like me? Is your name Olivia?"

"I had no choice!"

"Don't give me that bolox!"

"They had my brother baby. He got caught with a key in the boot of his car in Miami some time last year. It was either co-operate, or they were going to process him!"

"You dirty no good slag! That's the best part of half a million dollars you have nicked from me"

"I didn't know I was going to fall in love with you"

"So, the first time we met at the Clevelander was a set up? And Jorge?"

"He's my brother"

"Who's your handler?"

She whispered something under her breath I couldn't make out. Then she screamed...

"Stud!"

"What the fuck are you talking about?"

"The Italians get the gear from the Columbians and give it to Floyd. You do the rest. Stud picks it up from you!"

"Bollocks, I don't believe you!"

"Why do you think he had the car and the Rolex?"

I didn't want to believe it but, it made sense.

"It threw you off the scent!"

The room went deathly silent. Tony pulls his gun and tries to shoot Olivia, but it jammed. With rage in his eyes Donnie pulls his shooter, but I stand in front of Olivia and declare "I've got an idea!"

"Get out the fucking way or I'll shoot you too!"

Then Olivia screams, "He's undercover but he's turned!"

This changed everything. You can't kill policemen, even bent ones. "Trust me on this Tony, walk with me and I'll tell you what we are going to do"-

She bowed her head as she couldn't look me in the eye. I look at Tony and ask him to accompany me outside -

"When do you want me to move the gear?"

"You go tomorrow"!

"How much?"

"Fifty key"

"I'll speak to Junior and let him know.

"Do you still have friends on the force?"

"I do"-

We walk back in the room and Tony says "Let her go"-

121

"What about that cocksucker?"

"Fuck him, we've got plans"-

I had to come up with something that wasn't suspicious as I had made a song and dance about having some time off, so I played the old it's my mates leaving do in the Bahamas routine and I'm going to say goodbye. I got on the ship about seven, went straight to my cabin and devised a cunning plan.

I found Junior in the restaurant, "I need to speak to you!"

"I'll come down in a minute"

He didn't receive the news very well. He was happy with the plan, but my leaving was an issue. I explained I had to leave as we were in too deep but that once everything had settled down, I would be back in a years' time, give or take but look on the bright side, its fifty-grand your end. With a forced grin and a hug, he looked at me, "Let's do it!"

For a starter, my Italian associate turned up looking like something out of the Godfather. *Fucking ice-cream!* All heads in the restaurant turned to me as if to say, what are you doing with him? It wasn't rocket science. Then to make matters worse, we pulled up at the hotel next to the casino. I mean, let's advertise the fact what we are doing, but then it hit me. He or they didn't care as they had everyone in their pocket. Anyone else can jog on and jog on, they did. I quickly developed an, I don't give a fuck attitude as it seemed that I was untouchable. However, as in all these cases, I forgot about the monitors. There is always someone watching, who is watching someone else. There is both intel and counter-intel, which meant that someone somewhere had to have had eyes on me. I was in too deep to worry about it now because if I had been under surveillance for any length of time, then I was fucked, but I decided to play along anyway.

Inside the room, were Tony and Floyd.

"I believe you two know each other"!

"Grab those two bags and make sure it gets to Miami".

I never said a word. I picked up the sniff and sidled out the door straight to reception where Charles was waiting. We get to the port and hand Junior, the bags.

I get to Miami loaded, which the gate crew found funny, so they just waved me off. I get a taxi, and within ten minutes, I am back at my place on South Beach.

The next half an hour was going to dictate how I was going to live the rest of my life. If I get out of this, I will never do anything as dumb again. I will concentrate on making something of myself in the casino game.

At the port Junior loads the cocaine into the boot of Jorge's taxi. He then goes to pick up Olivia. Ten minutes later they are back at my apartment. "Call Stud and let him know to meet you at this address in Sarasota"-

"What? Why?"

"Because there's too much weight to handle on these premises"-

Olivia makes the call and in an excited tone I hear Stud say, "Fuck me!"

I couldn't even look at her, as if the truth be told I was in love. However, I secretly admired her for looking after her brother.

"You can keep the readies as well"-

"Sorry?"

Jorge didn't know he'd been rumbled as clearly Olivia hadn't told him.

"What the fuck is going on?"

"I know what you've done Jorge!"

He looked sheepish and didn't know what to say!"-

"There is fifty-kilo of cocaine in the boot of your car. Deliver it to Stud. Olivia, there is a hire car outside. Follow your brother but keep your distance"

"OK!"

"Now fuck-off!"

I walked in the bedroom listening to Olivia crying as they left, and I myself in bits!

About thirty minutes from Sarasota on the 75, Jorge sees flashing blue lights right beside him. He's instructed to pull over. Stud gets out, flashes his badge and pulls his shooter –

"Get out of the fucking car!"

Jorge recognises him and goes a funny colour. He opens the door with Studs gun in his face and holds his hands up. As

123

predicted, Stud jumps in and drives off. Less than sixty seconds later Olivia finds a frightened Jorge on the side of the 75.

"I don't know what the fuck's happening but get in" –

About five minutes up the road, they find a turn off, re-join the 75 and head back to Miami. Olivia….

"If I know David, I think they are going to fuck Stud"

"I don't care!"

"Do you have any money on you?"

"It's at the apartment?"

Like a bat-out-of-hell, Olivia drove to their apartment, packed lightly, picked up the money and passports and went straight to the airport.

At the same time, Stud and his entourage pull off the seventy-five, drive to a quiet spot and open the boot.

"What the fuck?"

He puts his hand into the bag and runs his fingers through the sand of Xanadu Beach. On top of the pile was a note that had printed in big bold letters *'FUCK YOU'!!!*

As he lifts his head to look at his colleague, he begins to hear the faint sound of a helicopter, "What the fuck?"

In less than sixty seconds the chopper has landed, and the Miami Police Department announce their arrival.

"Get on the ground!"

"I can explain"

With all four federal officers brandishing their weapons pointing them at Stud, they once again pronounce – "Get on the fucking ground!"

"I'm a cop!"

"You're under arrest!"

"What are you talking about?"

They open the car and underneath the passengers' front seat is a kilo of Columbia's finest, courtesy of one David Moynihan. The cop pulls a knife, slices it open and tastes the goods. "You're under arrest man!"

"But I'm a cop!"

"You were a cop!"

124

Ten minutes later there was another knock at the door, this time it was Kenneth, (Junior's brother) with the two bags of sniff. I instructed him to drive around the block for twenty minutes. The door goes again. It was Gio. He never said a word. He just stared at me, then he pulls his gun. He brings out a knife, cuts open one of the keys, samples the yayo and then says, "Enjoy New York"!
He picked up the bags and goes to walk out.
"Ain't you forgetting something?"
My end was five large a key. A quarter of a million dollars. Gio goes to his car with the cocaine and comes back with the money. I count out fifty and go and find Kenneth....
"Tell Junior I'll be back next year!"

19

I went to Tugboats to be met by my mate.

"What's going on"?

"What do you mean"?

"Why can't you go back to Freeport? You been a naughty boy"?

"I don't want to talk about it"!

"Have it your way. Your tickets at the airport. If I was you, I'd have a non-stop party for a few days! Trust me mate you'll love it"!

"Do you want a drink"?

"No, Monz, I got to go. Enjoy your trip"!

"Thanks".

"Take care, mind how you go"!

I hailed a cab for the airport. I can't believe what Olivia did to me but telling her to jog-on was the right thing to do. I had survived an unbelievable seven months but now it was time for a working vacation. I called my mate in Tampa to let him know I had some readies and to ask if he could keep hold of it for me. He arranged a flight, so we made a meet in New York the following day. Moreover, I had unfinished business in Miami, and I made a vow that it wouldn't be long before I was back.

1. The cruise of a lifetime.
2. The Summer of love.
3. David the Boxman.
4. Carnival Cruise Line.
5. Junior and Kenneth.
6. We're off and running.
7. Found Him.
8. RCCL.
9. Azure Seas
10. Monza on the March.
11. Sovereign of the Seas.
12. Greatest football team that ever sailed the seven seas.
13. I had to plan.
14. Atlantic City.
15. I'm the Boss.
16. Donnie and Gio.
17. Poker scam.
18. Bermuda.

'A speck of dust
on a celestial ball
that is me.
Found himself
in the place
he was born to be'

David Moynihan
Circa, December 2021

Part 2

1

Tom O'Sullivan, fourteen stone, six-foot-two, eyes are blue, strikingly handsome, assertive, some might say aggressive, but as far as he was concerned, these were the tools he created for success. As wide as the Hudson, he carried himself with real purpose. He was an old pal of mine from the east end. A real man about town that knew his biscuits. I booked into the Chelsea Hotel on 222 West 23rd Street, Manhattan in the heart of the meat-packing district. Steeped in American history, it was a throwback to modernism but in its current state it resembled a museum. I bought a coffee and bacon sandwich and waited. With basic civilities and a cynical and somewhat unfriendly attitude, we got business done quickly. I gave him two hundred large in stone-cold-readies -

"What you up to?"

"Going on a two-month cruise" –

"Someone's doing alright!"

"Don't ask" –

"OK mate, I can't hang about, got business to do and all that"

"Sweet, I'll call you after Christmas and let you know when I'm coming back"

"All good brother"

"Take care"

"You too!"

In the city that never sleeps, I was completely blown away. London is bigger with a larger population. However, the height, scale and sheer size of the buildings amazed me. I hailed a cab and made my way to Hell's Kitchen on the upper west side of Manhattan. I quickly checked into my room, freshened up and headed out for a walk to grab something to eat.

I found a small deli two blocks away and dined al-fresco, allowing me to people watch the commuters and passers-by in the hustle and bustle of the city streets. I soon realised everyone in New York was in some sort of hurry. I arrived from Florida an hour before, where the climate has a lot to do with how everyday life works, but New York was an entirely different animal. It felt like home, but on a larger scale.

The following week I was set to start work on the Canada Star. A cruise ship - at least twice the size of 'The Sun'. The itinerary was a step up from what I was used to. The cruise began with a weeklong voyage along the St. Lawrence River in Canada, followed by two weeklong cruises to Bermuda, before embarking on a twenty-one-day repositioning cruise from New York to New Orleans. Along the way, we stopped at Maryland, Philadelphia, North Carolina, South Carolina, Miami, Bahamas, Puerto Rico, Jamaica, Cozumel in Mexico, Aruba, Cartagena in Colombia, went through the Panama Canal, eventually arriving in Los Angeles, California. Finally, we finish in New Orleans, then a one-week cruise to Key West, Playa Del Carmen and an overnight stay in Cozumel. It felt like my cruise-day dreams were coming true, and I couldn't wait to get started.

The Canada Star had no previous experience of a dice table and, more importantly, how dice dealers work, so the company sent a supervisor on the first cruise to ensure we were compliant with the company's policies and procedures. The three other dice dealers and I had never been on a real cruise, so it was probably a wise thing to do.

Previously, we had worked on ships that were designed for gambling because, at the time, Florida was not in a betting jurisdiction. We were able to get off and on, with impunity. However, here it was different. We merry band of brothers were about to be trapped on a ship, which was not healthy for the rest of the crew. The Bermuda Star Line carried the elderly rather than youngsters in their twenties. It was a life of early nights and zero drama, which was about to change drastically over the course of next two months.

From the off, it was clear this was our chance to relax and recuperate after the wild months beforehand. Most days were at port, which meant we were not allowed to work as maritime law states you had to be in international waters to open. Each night we started around 9 pm after both dinner sittings and finish around 11pm as most of the clientele were in bed.

On our first cruise we set sail through the St. Lawrence River, in Canadian waters – which meant we couldn't work. Our supervisor, however, thought it best to open the casino. This was a disastrous mistake. For those who don't know, a ship pilot is responsible for the dock and departure of a ship from a port or harbour. He carries major influence in terms of how a ship operates regarding the opening of shops and casinos. Whilst he is on board, you cannot open. So, it came as somewhat of a surprise when he declared during a hand of blackjack that he was the pilot and to cease trading immediately. The captain was soon informed of our faux-pas and the pilot ordered the ship to return to port. This was extremely troublesome. On arrival at shore, we were greeted with several police officers readily waiting with handcuffs and marched off to jail.

We thought that was the end, but during the evening, the CEO of our company flew to New York to try and establish what had occurred. We cried foul. I would have declared I had done it if I did, but I was not in a position of authority to make that decision. None of us were and what was proving increasingly frustrating was the perpetrator had still not owned up. By now, the captain was on the scene with steam coming out of his ears. He wanted blood, and by the look on his face, it was mine he smelt. He demanded to know who was responsible for holding up his itinerary. "It was me", declared the individual responsible. Relief all around as she was subsequently marched off, never to be seen again.

Talk about making an impression. We were instant celebrities, rock stars amongst the ship's fraternity. It turns out that it wasn't only our department that was off, as quite a few of the crew were in the bar awaiting our arrival. I have never sought or been searching for fame, but I very quickly got the feel and flavour of its perks. Many of the crew were young, but there was no form of amusement onboard to keep them entertained. They had resigned themselves to the fact that it was a ship designed for a particular dynamic whose idea of a night out didn't exactly match theirs. So, they learned to live with it. That night we partied like no other, it was the stuff of legend, and this was our first night. The rest of the week was more of the same, party, bed, party. If truth be told, I was looking forward to the Bermuda cruise and three days off.

And as luck would have it, it was even better than expected. Bermuda is considered by the English as the last bastion of etiquette. A jewel in the crown of all the exotic locations (tax havens), the empire owns. It retains a lot of rules that some in this country would consider antiquated and archaic. However, that adds to the allure. Pink/white sand on the beaches, all add to the mystique of these beautiful little islands. In fact, they are so prim and proper that a dancer girlfriend of mine was dressed in a G-string on a beach when we were approached by what I thought was a tramp. Because of his accent, I couldn't understand what he was saying, so I told him to jog on. He then pulled a pass out of his pocket with the words 'beach patrol' and informed us if she did not get dressed in an appropriate fashion, we would be arrested.

Moving swiftly on, we were docked on Front Street in the capital Hamilton for three days which gave us an ideal position for entertainment purposes. We were in the Robin Hood pub when I made a fatal mistake. In the middle of the bar hangs a large bell. There is a sign on the wall that states if you ring said bell, you are obliged to buy everyone a drink. So, whilst you endeavour to purchase a libation or two, the bar staff ignore you. A tactic to get you to fall for their cunning plan. Muggings here fell for it, hook line and sinker. Ringing that bell cost me an arm and a leg. However, watching the bar team in action was a source of great hilarity. It was astonishing how many punters fell for it.

Bermuda came and went, then New York for three days before we set sail for the Caribbean. My powers of recollection are somewhat blurred around this time as the twenty-one-day repositioning cruise was one long party. Don't get me wrong, I recall being in Philly and the east coast, but I never came to until we landed in LA. So, after we eventually got to our home port in New Orleans, I only managed four weeklong cruises and felt it was time to come home. The fact it was Christmas also became a crucial deciding factor in the equation. However, I feel it is imperative to relate a little insight into those four fantastic weeks.

New Orleans is some city. You immediately identify why they have a carnival here. I would strongly recommend you give this place a visit, particularly if you like Jazz. We departed New Orleans at 7 pm Saturday, embarking on seven-day cruises that consisted of a sea day on Sunday, Key West (Florida) Monday, Playa del Carmen (Mexico) Wednesday, and overnight stay in Cozumel (Mexico). before arriving in New Orleans early Saturday morning. The stuff of dreams.

I had been to Ibiza several times, but Key West has to be the funkiest little island I have had the good fortune to visit. A real trend-setter's guide in how to relax. A throwback to yesteryear in its approach but uber trendy at the same time. It was 1987, but if someone had said it was 1957, you would have believed them.

Sea days were fun because they were akin to a day off. Back in those days, the average age of the clientele was of an elderly dynamic. To accentuate that point, one week we had to use the fridges in the kitchen as the morgue was at capacity. Subsequently, these clientele didn't play in the casino, so we just sat around playing with each other, literally.

Wednesday and Playa del Carmen were our favourites. This is where we really got to misbehave. Unbelievable beaches, fantastic cheap food and even cheaper booze. A young single person's dream. We departed at 5pm and arrived in Cozumel around 5.30pm for an overnight stay. We were off the ship at about 5.31, as this is where the fun really began. Carlos and Charlie's to begin with, then to any number of bars/clubs. From an economic perspective, it was a club goers dream. I didn't want it to end, but I was craving London for all intents and purposes. I wanted to go home as a London boy am I. I wanted to wash Olivia out of my hair. So, armed with ten large, a suntan and a suitcase full of memories, I came home. It was the 23rd of December, and I was due to return at the end of February to join the Discovery in Fort Lauderdale.

2

There is something about big cities that only people who come from big cities understand. Nowhere in the world takes the piss, better than us. It doesn't matter where we are but, home is home. It is where you belong. I fitted straight back in as if I hadn't been away. On my first night back, I was invited to a party at a casino bash where I made a reacquaintance of a casino manager pal of mine. One thing led to another, and after a large consumption of alcohol, he offered me my old job back on much improved terms. I said yes instantly. He made me promise that I would give him a year, as being a dice dealer, he knew we were a well sought-after commodity.

I got through Christmas, New Year, had a week off, started training and playing for Feltham in the Isthmian League and went back to work with relish. Charlie Chesters, smoke-filled rooms full of Chinamen, dice in the air, aggressive punters, aggressive dice dealers, SOHO. God, it was good to be home. I had another year's worth of experience behind me, so I got promoted to Boxman after the next round of Bahamian recruitment. I concluded that dice was as close to a football game without being a game of football. Charge, counter charge, banter, us against them and I got paid for doing it. Walking downstairs to take over the day shift was akin to walking out of a tunnel to play a game of football. You could feel the energy. It gave me butterflies. I had Tuesday/Wednesday off, which allowed me to play semi-pro football. I was being paid handsomely alongside my full-time job. No matter where we played, I always managed to make it back to Soho. Even though I had only been gone a year, you could see and feel the difference in this little part of London. The police were on a mission to clean it up, which they accomplished in a relatively short period of time. Gone went the sex shops, et al. In its place came trendy bars and boutiques, the likes of which are still prevalent today.

Ecstasy and cocaine were the mainstays of the underbelly in London. Along with the acid house scene, London was constantly throbbing to the beat of House Music. Big clubs became the norm alongside the summer of love in Ibiza in 88. DJs were the new rock stars, as they knew how to manipulate, cajole and excite a crowd. Alongside my pals, we thoroughly enjoyed the London scene and threw ourselves at it with gusto. It was a considerably favourable time to be alive. The problem I had was the constant questions about Miami, but I swerved them as I gave them a load of fanny!

After six months I called Tom. "I thought you'd forgotten me?"

"Sorry mate I've been busy!"

"Don't apologise mate, it's your money!"

"Anyway, all good"

"Double sweet here son!" –

"I'll be over soon"

"Let me know and I'll pick you up at the airport!"

"Sweet, take care!"

"Look forward to seeing ya, mind ow ya go"

Work was going well. I had established myself as a Boxman now. Even though Chesters was considered small compared to the rest of the casinos in London, what it lacked in size, we made up in our personalities.

I thoroughly enjoyed working on a Saturday night as this was when the action exploded. The dice table was steaming. Both ends had at least eight players with place bets, come bets, don't come bets, front line bets with full and partial odds, prop bets that were off the scale, there was even some Herbert playing the field, but then (there is always one), it was proper going off. The game ebbed and flowed with a three-time twelve on the come out. The stickman was sweating his bollocks off, the basemen were going like the clappers, and there was me right in the thick of it. "Bring that back, put that back, how much"? This was what it was all about. If there is anything that creates as much excitement as a local derby or a great DJ at a rave, dice was it. Loud, raucous, and uber aggressive, it was fun. It was technically difficult to deal, but I was a natural.

It was a sophisticated form of penny-up-the-wall played by shysters that took part in illegal poker games at spielers owned by gangsters. These were my people. I knew them. I understood their ilk. I was meant to do this. I looked after the boys. They

134

looked after me. It was the ultimate team experience. A dice game is dealt at a speed that is relevant to its slowest dealer. Therefore, it is imperative that the team is in sync. You can't move the bones until you are comfortable that all bets have been explained and understood. It's a game of relentless speed. It is the most exciting casino game by a country mile, but alas, it is dying in this country.

3

We were getting towards the end of the season when something started to bug me. I had unfinished business in Miami. I had done the year I promised Brian. So, after a particularly cold night in March, I got home, rolled a joint and put the radio on. After about ten minutes, an advert came on. It was the sound of the sea hitting the shore, you know the type. They use these meditation tapes by way of a calming influence. I was high when suddenly, the sweetest female voice I have ever heard in my life uttered the immortal words, "Miami". "Heathrow to Miami £99 return". I couldn't get on the phone to British Airways quick enough.

I was absolutely buzzing by the time I put the phone down as I had two-hundred thousand reasons to be happy. I rang Tom in Tampa to tell him the news. A voice I was unfamiliar with answered the phone,

"Hello?"

"Is Tom there?"

"Who?"

I got a sinking feeling, blood rushed to my face, and I suddenly felt very sick. "May I speak to Tom please?"

"There's no-one here by that name"

"Tom O'Sullivan has lived there for more than three years. Is that 813 215 8732?"

"It is. We moved in three months ago, if that helps"

I read out the address.

"That's us, but I can assure you he doesn't live here anymore!" –

"Did he leave a forwarding address?"

"Never met him, but I can give you the number of the agent"

"Thank you"

With a heavy heart I knew I done me bollocks! I called the agent. "I'm calling regarding a client of mine, a Mr. Tom O'Sullivan who was renting the house at this address. Do you have any details of his forwarding address?"

"I'm familiar with the address, but that name doesn't ring a bell. Hold the line I'll check for you! –

Fucking knew it!!! She came back on the phone,

"Hello, the name I have is Geoff Peck, or *Pecky* as he insisted on being called!"

I gave her a description.

"That's him! If you find him, can you ask him to give me a call"

"I was going to say the same thing to you. Is everything OK?"

"I can't discuss that with you as it's a private matter, but we are more than keen to speak with him"!

"OK will do!" –

The sick fuck had done a bunk with me readies, which I didn't understand as he was swimming in money. I'm going to Miami anyway. I'm sure there's a more than reasonable explanation.

4

I flew to Miami, in search of Tom. However, I had more chance of getting a wank off the .... So, I reserved a room on the beach and topped-up my tan for a week. Then by virtue of my dice dealing skills, I got a job with Carnival Cruise Lines as a dealer onboard the Celebration.

The casino had four dice, four roulette, twenty blackjack tables as well as five hundred slots. It was a money-making machine. The casino was positioned so the clients had to walk past or through when they finished dinner enroute to the show lounge. It was a brilliant strategy, simple by design but extremely effective. This was my first experience of how casinos should be run on ships in terms of the games on offer, but the problem was most of the crew could barely speak English. And as this was the eighties, most of the passengers had never been to a real casino before. They were not familiar with the mechanics of how a casino worked, and the crew were not familiar with young American culture. It was a recipe for success, as it gave me an opportunity to get a fundamental understanding of the marketing and management of how to drive business and create footfall.

Carnival's basic strategy was they had a captive audience full of a much younger dynamic than other cruise lines. Fill the casino with young women, run educational games of how dice, blackjack, roulette and three-card Caribbean stud were played, make the minimums small enough to entice them in and there you have it. It was a real 'build it, and they will come' scenario, and it worked.

Another aspect of how Carnival operated was they advertised all over Europe looking for cashiers with the promise of life on board a cruise ship, so there was no need for experience. No need for prior cash handling or the essential component of the language. All you had to have, was looks. Once they got a basic grip of English, they were trained to deal casino games. The crew had never seen a dealer like me before, and I stress it was not because I was captain fantastic. I was trained properly and dealt the game differently, that was all. This got in me into all sorts of favourable positions. The only issue I had was with the supervisors who couldn't keep up. It wasn't their fault as they were alien to the game, so I had to explain to them what I was doing a lot of the time because an aspect of dealing dice was there were a lot of tricky or rascally moves you could use to maintain speed and momentum.

The marketing department aimed at a much younger dynamic than all the other cruise lines, with the average age in their late twenties. If you were young and single, this was the holiday of a lifetime.

I met a young lady based in Miami. I had a week's vacation booked, so we thought it was a good idea to stay with her rather than fork out for a hotel. This was a good move. She lived right on the beach in what can only be described as an archetypal Floridian beach dwelling. Two nights into my holiday Carla and I were strolling along South Beach, found a restaurant, ordered some drinks and proceeded to people watch, when who should walk to our table. Donnie and Gio, the I-ties. We made introductions, engaged in small talk before he gave me his number with a promise to call him. As they were leaving, my date looked at me and remarked, "How the fuck do you know them".

"You don't want to know",

"Oh yes, I do. They look like something out of the mob".

"Exactly, that's why you don't want to know" -

By the end of the week, I was going to resign and spend more time in Miami. Carla offered me a place to stay with her whilst I found my own place. This lifted the pressure as now I could enjoy my last cruise.

As I had resigned, I got the week off so I could travel as a passenger. This was not good for my liver. A case of beer in the crew bar cost four dollars, a glass of Budweiser twenty-five cents, a single shot fifty cents, it was an alcoholic's dream. I was glad when it was over. I simply couldn't look at or taste any more alcohol. On Saturday morning at 10 am, I went through immigration, disembarked straight into the arms of Carla. I don't know whether it was the fact that I was finished or the sight of a beautiful woman, but I had a sense of euphoria tinged with excitement. I was going to relax for a couple of weeks before resuming my career as a small-time hood.

Carla had an apartment on 3rd and Ocean, right in the heart of South Beach. The location was perfect as we were based in the heart of the action. Carla worked in the modelling world as a freelance photographer and being self-employed allowed her to work as she pleased. We decided to spend some real-time together to see if we got on, rather than the usual scenario of realising that it was just a cruise ship thing.

South Beach had changed. When I first arrived three years earlier, it was gritty, a little untidy – downright dangerous in some places. Now, it was trendy bars, clubs, boutiques that charged ridiculous prices for their clobber, cafes that charged ridiculous prices for their food, a smattering of modelling agencies. What was once the hub of the Cuban Latino community was now the playground of the rich and famous. Miami was uber-trendy. This was to work in my favour as Carla had access to the happening crowd. We went to all the best parties, which provided me with some useful connections. We were happy to carry on with the living arrangement, as I paid half the rent. The two weeks came and went, so it was time to go to work.

5

You must be very careful where these things are concerned as people like Floyd are protected. It is one of the most corrupt places on earth, so in the negotiation stage, you go through a game of give and take. "What can I do for you?"

"What happened after I left?"

"There was a shit storm! Stud took it on the chin, if you can believe that?"

"What do you mean?"

"Turns out, he had a lot of previous. They had him bang to rights kid. He's in the system in bum-fuck Idaho or somewhere!"

"Olivia and Jorge?"

"Let that slide, David!"

"Just asking?"

"They flew south, same time you went to New York" –

"How do you know all this?"

"It's my business to know!" –

"Are you still active on the boats?"

"No, we let them use the Islands and they pay us in kind. And anyway, my connections in Miami won't do business with them!"

"Is this where I step in?"

"Are your routes still open?"

"Don't know yet, I'll find out this week" –

"If you can open them, I would be more than happy to do business with you David!"

"Are you still on the same number?"

"No, here's my new one!"

"Give me a couple of days"

"Look forward to it" -

We had a hearty Bahamian lunch, agreed a price, and exchanged pleasantries. Now all I had to do was find Junior. On the way to the airport, I formulated a strategy. My role in these transactions would consist of nothing but collecting the readies. Risk versus reward. I take no risk but receive a lot of rewards. It seemed like an attractive proposition to me.

The next day Carla and I booked a cruise to the Bahamas on the 'Scandinavian Sun.' I didn't inform Carla of my nefarious intentions. We settled by the pool, ordered a drink and I went to work. As I enter the restaurant, his voice can be heard bellowing across the room, "David, is that really you?"

"Alo mate. I told you I was coming back" –

"Yeah, but they all say that"

"How are you, Junior?"

"I'm all the better for seeing you!"

"I need to talk to you!"

"When?"

"Now!"

"Come inside here"

We find a little space, next to the restaurant,

"Do you want to start work?"

"Do you remember my brother Kenneth?"

"Yes, I do!"

"He has a green card now and he's living in Miami. He helps me in what am I doing on here. The same as before I met you" –

"Saves me a job!"

"When do you want to start?"

"It will take me a few days to sort out, then I'll be in touch"

"Great, I'll stop what I'm doing so we can make some real money!"

"Take care!"

"Really good to see you David, really good!"

We get to Freeport, and I go directly to see Floyd.

"That was quick!"

"Now's as good a time as any!"

"Precisely!"

"Does your driver still work for you?"

"He most certainly does" –

"We go tomorrow, same as before. Drop the gear with Junior, he'll do the rest" –

As soon as Carla and I arrive at Pier One I make excuses and ask the barman if I can use the phone –

"Yeah?"

"Donnie, it's David, meet me tonight at The Clevelander, at midnight on the beach!"

He never even answered, just put the phone down.

I get back on the ship, go to the restaurant and give Junior the good news.

"Thank you, David!"

"By the way, you get fifteen hundred per key, your brother gets five hundred!"

"I look forward to working with you again!"

"Tell Kenneth to get it to the Marriott before midnight. I'll be in the foyer" –

South Beach at sunset really is a sight for sore eyes. It is the best place in the world to people watch as there are more models per square inch, than anywhere else in the world. If you are a little body conscious, this is not the place for you as both males and females are of equal beauty. Yes, there is a lot of plastic around, but that is to be expected in the land of the rich and beautiful. I like Miami, even with all the pretentious wannabees, warts and all. It's fun, it's funky, it's alive. On any given night, the walk along the beach can make you feel like a movie star as the sound of a Latino beat gets a grip of you.

Around midnight, the boys Donnie and Gio turn up, so I go outside and jump in the back of the motor,

"Alo chaps" –

"It's the fucking Englishman!"

"How are ya?"

"Good, how's business!"

"This time it's watertight. Makes sense to go again!"

"You got balls; I'll give you that!"

"The difference is I have a room at the Marriott, Key Biscayne. You and only you two come over tomorrow at midnight and I'll have two kilos of pure cocaine for you"

"How much?"

"Ten large a key!"

They turned around in stereo with these quizzical looks.

"The price on the street has gone up forty per-cent in the last eighteen months boys. You can afford it!"

"Fucking English cocksucker!"

"Is it the same with Floyd?"

"What?"

"You sort out Floyd, right?"

143

Once again, they both turned around, so I nodded and got out the car. "See you tomorrow boys!"

There is a myth surrounding sniff and the mob. It was alleged they were not involved in the movement of said commodity as if you got caught the sentences were so long, therefore, you were more than likely going to fold under questioning. However as fifty per cent of the world's cocaine consumption is in the states, there was way too much money to be made, and if there is one thing these boys knew what to do. *It was making money!*

"I'm jogging-on boys!"

They both just stared at me. I don't care who you are or, how tough you are, but there is something extremely menacing about these types of characters.

6

We were off and running. As we had a lot of success with the previous operation, we used the same MO. It worked a treat. We were making a lot of money, so I moved out of Carla's for obvious reasons. In the first instance because of the seriousness of my business and second, I wasn't going to get caught out again. She understood the rules, I was twenty-five, and doing alright for me self when I got a shock. I was eating al-fresco at the News Café when he bound across the road. With a massive grin,

"Don't get up!"

"Fancy seeing you here!"

"I've come to see you" –

"This ain't good!"

"Yes and no" –

"He wants to increase the loads?" –

"Yes, but he has something that will interest you!"

"I'm making him fortunes. Why run the risk of fucking it all up?"

"And what about you David?"

"What about me, Floyd?"

"You're making more than forty large a week!"

"And?"

"Be very careful here David. Don't use the fact they like you. You could get seriously hurt. Anyway, he wants to see you!"

"When?"

"Now!"

"Right now?"

"Right now!"

He wasn't happy. He never was. He gave his side of the story, and I gave mine. He expressed a desire to double the load, and I felt it wasn't worth the risk.

Why change a winning formula. Everyone was winning. I explained he benefited most of all as he gave precisely fuck all to the transaction. This was not well received. When you are young and full of cum, you often make mistakes as it's a part of the process. And this was as big a mistake as I could make. He explained there wouldn't be an operation, if it wasn't for him, as working with his lot meant no one overstepped the mark. I suddenly realised there was a sinister edge in his voice, a threatening tone which instantly made me feel uncomfortable. I knew I fucked up. You don't talk to people like him like I just did. I'm not talking about getting caught with your pants down by your missus or coming home drunk and pissing in the cupboard trouble. I am talking life-threatening trouble. The kind of trouble where you go missing. There was only one solution to this, and that was to agree to his proposal.

"Before you go"

"Sorry?"

"Donnie, what was the name of that cocksucker?"

"O'Sullivan!"

"Tom O'Sullivan?" says I –

"That's him. I believe you're looking for him?"

"And?"

"We found him; this is his address. Up-market place in West Palm Beach!"

"May I have it please?"

"You're a smart kid, so Donnie and Gio are going to take you!"

"When?"

"Tonight. They'll pick you up at ten, be ready!"

"Thank you, Tony!"

We shook hands and agreed on a meet next week to ensure I had finalised our new plan. FUCK!

This was not good. On top of that, Carla was starting to become suspicious as I hadn't worked in nearly three months, but I always paid for lunch and dinner and never seemed to mention money. It was slowly coming on top. I got away with it up to this point, but lunch and dinner in Miami was not cheap, especially as we frequented the nicer establishments. Lunch could easily cost two hundred dollars, with dinner costing two or three times that and considering we ate out three or four times a week, you could understand why she was getting uneasy. I had to come up with a new plan and quickly. Work was a no-no as I didn't have a green card. I had a ninety-day visa which I could

146

extend by flying to the Bahamas as this was considered international.

7

As arranged the boys were outside at ten looking extremely professional. This was their world; how they lived. As easy as I deal a game of dice, they would put someone in the ground, it was second nature.

It's about an hour's drive to West Palm from Miami. As soon as we pull into the estate the boys clicked into gear. They started straightening up their clothes and both checked their side-arm. This was getting serious! Donnie stays in the car whilst Gio and I go knock on his door.

"Give me your shooter!"

"You ever used one before?"

"Yes!"

"The boss said we were to handle it!"

"It was my two-hundred large!"

"Fair enough, but if the boss asks!?!"

Gio raps the door. There are footsteps on the wooden floor. My heart is akin to having drunk half-a-dozen Red Bulls. There is a whistling sound, the latch is let free, and the door opens. I front kick-it and knock him flying, Gio is on him like a flash. He's got him in a choke hold, and I push the gun in his face ……

"Where is he?"

"Who?"

"Don't give me that bollocks!"

"I don't know what you're talking about?"

I shove the shooter in his mush, "I'm gonna ask you one more time!"

"I don't know what you're talking about!"

Gio says "Shoot this motherfucker!"

I wasn't going to shoot him, I just wanted to put the frightener's up him, also Gio is strangling him so tight that he can't get his words out -

"You got one more chance!"

"He's done a moonlight!"

"To where?"

"Ain't got a Danny, said he won't be coming back! He left two weeks ago" -

"If you see him, tell him I want me readies. He knows!"

"Who shall I say called?"

"Monza!"

"So, you're Monza!"

"What does that mean?"

"I've heard a lot about you" –

"And you?"

"Pecky!"

Five foot ten, eight-and-a-half-stone soaking wet. He had a dodgy scouse perm and a tache akin to a Swedish porn-star from the same era. Disappointment didn't do it justice –

"Tell that slaggy faced mug to call me!" You're the bane of my life! Pecky this, Pecky that! I thought you'd be bigger!"

"They all say that. Anyway, what the fuck are you doing with that lot?"

"Don't ask. I can't hang about. Got to go son, let's have a light ale some time? Before I go, you looking for work?"

"I'm always looking for a bit of work".

"Sweet, take care!"

"Listen, before you go, he's in Florida. Told me he's running card scams or something!"

I get in the car …….

"Who the fuck was that guy?"

"Not the geezer we were looking for!"

The sniff was making me paranoid. I was permanently high. I could see the receptionists eyeing me with contempt. It was on the edge of their tongues. How could I afford two hundred and fifty bucks a night for a month? I used whores frequently. I was starting to lead a drug dealer's lifestyle. I was turning into something I absolutely hated. So, one morning after a three-day coke and sex fest, I decided I had had enough. Moreover ….

Junior came to see me highly agitated. "Something's not right!"

"What do you mean?"

"I always have someone watching me!"

"What?"

"When I pick up, I have one guy on the deck and one following me, to keep an eye out!"

"And?"

"And today I was followed!"

"What did they look like?"

"Feds David, fucking Feds!"

"Are you sure?"

"100 per cent!"

I call Floyd ....

In a very strange tone, he say's "Junior has all the details, I'm afraid our business is done here!"

There is another voice –

"Who's this?"

This was the nail in the coffin I was looking for. The excuse I could go missing. I shut the operation down immediately. We got away with importing cocaine on a major scale for six months with no drama, so it was time to walk. Time to inform the Italian.

He was not happy because his end meant there was no jail time if it went tits-up, but as before, he accepted my explanation that no one got nicked, we all made good money, but it was time to move on. We booked a table at a well-known ridiculously overpriced restaurant that only in Miami do they seem to get away with. He called his wife, and I took a chance in calling Carla and extending an invitation to dinner. Surprisingly she accepted.

It took my breath away when she turned up. She was truly beautiful both inside and out. The four of us had a blast, and for a second, I thought it might not be such a bad idea if I stayed, but the better side of me told me to be thankful I had survived.

We had a great time. His wife was a real character who thought all Englishmen spoke like James Bond. She was from the Bronx and could not understand a word I said. It was hilarious watching her trying to repeat my lines. A night of much hilarity. I had never seen that side of him before because I didn't want to. We finished our drinks and said our goodbyes. I shook his hand with real vigour as I had made a friend for life. He motioned for me to give him a hug which I did. We had a moment of mutual respect. Even though I would return to Miami, I never saw him again. Whenever I see a movie of that type of genre, it always brings back fond memories of our time together. My only concern is that in his line of business, I would hazard a guess he is not doing particularly well. I genuinely hope I am wrong, but the lifestyle speaks for itself. The next time I am in Miami, my friend, I shall raise a glass for you.

Back to Carla.

We found a bar on the beach. We laughed, cried, we talked at great length of what might have been, but we knew it was over. With a feeling of respect and deep lust, I suggested a dance, she suggested we go back to her place. I lost. She only lived around the corner in a small block of apartments on the first floor. By the time we got to her door, we were both practically naked.

It was tough in the morning. I must have said goodbye five times, but when you have a deep respect for someone, it is a difficult thing to do. She knew I had to leave for my own good, as did I, so we made a solemn promise that she would come to England in six months to see me. This never materialised. They never do. It is best they don't, as you never get back those intense feelings. It is, therefore, best you leave with your memories and a smile on your face.

I stayed in Miami for a couple more days to hide the readies. I gave Gio a number in London to call if by some miracle he found O'Sullivan! I booked my flight, said my goodbyes with a promise I would be back in a couple of years.

7

The Victoria Sporting Club on Edgware Road, London, housed the biggest and best dice games in the world in 1990. If you wanted to prove that you were a part of the elite in the dice world, then there was no bigger stage to prove it on. 'The Vic', as it is affectionately known, had two dice tables, one three-pound and one five-pound minimum. There were three dice games in London at the time, Charlie Chesters, The Sportsman and The Vic. Chesters was a great place to learn by virtue of the consistent small action and the insistence of the box men to adhere to procedures. The Sportsman was a step up from that in terms of action, but 'The Vic' was just big boy shit. It was relentless, night after night, bet after bet, press after press, come bet after come bet, prop bet centre action the likes of which the world has never seen and will never see again.

Everything I had heard about The Vic was true. It was a massive step up from Chesters, a well-oiled machine, but it had to be because of the action. I didn't really get it at the time because we were cocooned on the craps tables, but it was a great learning curve that I would lean on later in my career.

I was about two years in now, and even though I loved dice with a passion, I was yearning for something more. I wanted to go in the pit and concentrate on the other games, but because of my so-called dice expertise, I was refused. Then like a bolt out of the blue, the reason I had been looking for, just happened.

I had clearly had enough, when a pal of mine said he had the number for RCCL (Royal Caribbean Cruise Lines).

"You got it on you"?

"1-800-casino. Wait till you get home as you need to call international"!

In a fit of pique, I grabbed one of the payphones and dialled the number. To my astonishment, there was an answer.

"Hello, Royal Caribbean".

"Hi, my name is David Moynihan, and I would like to apply for a job as a dealer with your company".

"How did you get this number, David? It is only used by people that work for us"!

"Sorry about that, shall I call back later"?

"Now that you are on the phone, I might as well take some details. What do you deal and for how long"?

"I have dealt blackjack and roulette for seven years".

"We have a slight problem here, David, in that we have a waiting list of about eighteen months".

"I have also dealt dice for seven years"!

"Where are you working at the moment"?

"The Vic".

"Can you hold the line please, David"?

"I can".

A male voice suddenly appears.

"Hi David, I'm David, too".

As luck would have it, this guy had worked at The Vic for four years, albeit some considerable time before me. He seemed impressed, "How much notice do you have to give"?

"Have I got the job"?

"You most certainly have".

"One week"!

"Good, call us back tonight, and I will give you the details"!

Just like that, I had got a job on a break, no interview, no table test. Such was the respect for dice dealers from The Vic that we were given jobs because of our reputation. I bounced back into the breakroom, went through the double doors onto the floor, got hold of the stick and declared in a loud audible voice, "That's me, I'm orf"!

"Just call the fucking game, Monz", said the Boxman.

"You get one weeks' notice. Hand me one of those roulette cards and a pen, please"!

"You getting me at it, Monz"?

"No!".

The Boxman handed me the relevant materials, and I resigned on a roulette card. I wrote the day's date; 'I hereby give you one weeks' notice' and signed it. Boom, I was done. I was immediately dragged off the game and into the manager's office. My mate Chris Shuter was waiting for me,

"What's the problem"?

"There is absolutely no problem".

"Don't tell lies. It is written all over your fucking face".

"OK, now that you ask. I believe I can have a career in the casino business, but if I stay here, I won't get a shot at the title. There are a lot of people that have far more casino experience than I; however, I believe I possess a different skill set to them, and if I was given an opportunity, I could prove it".

"I never saw that coming".

"There are a lot of solid professionals at this club whom all deserve a chance at management. You do the fundamentals right; you have good people in the right positions. The club is very well run. If I was to wait for my chance, it would probably take twenty years".

"Fair enough, do you want to work your notice"?

"Not if I don't have to"!

"OK, clear out your locker, bring us back your uniform, and then you can jog on"!

As I left the premises, Chris was waiting for me.

"What are you going to do"?

"Going back on the ships".

"Miami"?

"Yes, mate".

"Fucking love Miami"!

"I'm buzzing already"!

"Take care".

"And you, my friend"!

"Listen, Monz, if ever you want to come back here, don't hesitate to call us. You can have your job back anytime"!

He didn't need to say that, but it made me feel good. It was a good piece of management because instead of leaving with a feeling of frustration, I felt like a million dollars. Now let's get down the pub.

Soon as I got in there, my mate Too Tall Terry and his brother Chris were on me.

"Did you really resign on a roulette card"?

"Yes, I did".

I was proud of myself, but on reflection and with the benefit of hindsight, it was a dumb thing to do. Looking back, I was hurt that I didn't get the back-up I thought I deserved, but thirty years later, I now realise it was an horrendous way to behave. Petulant, immature, even downright disrespectful. If I had an opportunity, I would grab hold of that kid and tell him he was wrong to act in such an inappropriate fashion. I would tell him to go and apologise to all and sundry and inform them that it would never happen again.

. . . .

To say I liked the states would be an understatement. I was in my late twenties now, so I knew deep down that this was going to be the trip that either made or broke me. I had decided that I was going to relax on the first contract, take it nice and easy and work my way in slowly. I had mastered dealing, I was considered an expert on dice, and I had experience as an Inspector in the pit. More importantly, I had real gambling-related skills by virtue of my penny-up-the-wall, greyhound racing, poker dealing and working as a settler all before I was eighteen. I had what no one else possessed. I had a deep understanding of the players. I could relate to them; I spoke their language. Whatever part of society you came from didn't matter to me as I knew how to show the right amount of empathy in a loss or, conversely, the knowing wink or a little smile when they won. It was now time to test those skills, to see if I had that little bit extra that could get me into management.

It was late June, so I had a week to get ready for my next instalment of whatever the Southeast of the states and the Caribbean had to offer. This was going to be my last gig on the boats. It was a young man's game, and all things considered, I had developed the right mindset. I had booked an early flight that enabled me to have three days in Fort Lauderdale. I arrived on Wednesday before joining the Azure Seas, one of the older ships of a fast-growing fleet that had the biggest cruise ship in the world. I was excited. I said the relevant goodbyes and went to see certain people because I genuinely didn't know If I was ever coming back. More importantly, I said goodbye to Nan. It didn't matter how excited I was. It was always difficult saying farewell to her. She was my rock, was Esther Power.

I took one last trip to Cooke's Pie & Mash on the Goldhawk Road. Double pie, double mash and liquor, loads of pepper and vinegar, *Food of the Gods*! Washed down with a nice cup of 'Rosie-Lee', I was once more off to Miami and the best three years of my life.

8

I joined the *Azure Seas* the last year it was in service. An ocean-going liner of some twenty thousand tonnes, it was originally built in 1955 in Northern Ireland. She was the first cruise ship to be named by a reigning British monarch (Queen Elizabeth II) and was my introduction to a cruise line that had an aggressive expansion strategy. Three months beforehand, she was doing three-and four-day cruises out of Los Angeles to San Diego, to Ensenada (Mexico) and Santa Catalina, an island off the coast of LA, but because of the success of the Sovereign of the Seas, she was rebirthed to Fort Lauderdale to sail the same itinerary as the Sovereign just a day later whose home port was Miami. We departed on Sunday, had a sea day Monday, Labadee (Haiti) Tuesday from 7 am – approx. 3 pm, San Juan (Puerto Rico) from 10 am – 2 am Wednesday-Thursday, St Thomas on Thursday from 7 am – 5 pm, and then two sea days Friday and Saturday. The passengers disembarked in Fort Lauderdale on Sunday morning early before we set sail again at approximately 5 pm to start the whole process again. *It was absolutely magical.*

As she was now an old lady, the Azure had some redeeming features that I would never have the pleasure of seeing again. The cabins had floor beds which was handy because if you were on the top bunk, it was a right old palaver getting up there lagging. The number of times that I had embarrassing scenarios attempting to get my latest squeeze into and up the ladder that led to the top bunk were far too many to mention. The girls used to pull their dresses up, exposing their knickers to all and sundry, giving the bottom bunk a right eye-full and about ten minutes later a full running commentary of what was occurring approximately two to three feet below. Forget the old saying that goes, 'what happens in Vegas, stays in Vegas'. It should read 'what happens on a cruise ship, stays on a cruise ship'. We had a porthole and a built-in wardrobe, an ensuite shower room and enough space to have a staff party. All-in-all a cracking result. I had dinner in the officer's mess, then made my way to the casino for my first night as a dealer on board the Azure Seas.

Considering the ship was small in stature, the casino was tastefully done. Over two floors, we had a dice/craps table, four blackjacks, one three-card Caribbean stud poker and one roulette table. We also housed approximately one hundred slot machines and took the passengers that couldn't get on The Sovereign because of various reasons. It was perfect for my strategy of sailing around the Caribbean doing fuck all for months and getting laid with some attractive women in the process.

After some very basic introductions, I was assigned a blackjack table, shuffled the cards and started dealing. It was bliss. I was in full conversation with the passengers, offering them tips on where to go and what to do and giving them the full rundown on Puerto Rico. I informed them it was a beautiful island but a particularly tricky place to visit as the crime rate was through the roof. If you want to see a beach – use the hotels as the public beaches were somewhat hostile. Be very careful in San Juan after dark as you will be OK up to a certain point but don't stray a lot further from the Small World bar or Lazer's and don't get into unlicensed cabs, the usual stuff we were aware of by virtue of experience. However, this did not apply to me as I fucking loved San Juan because it was a real den of iniquity. Yes, you had to be careful, but if you carried yourself correctly and deployed an, I don't give a fuck attitude, they left you alone. Because of my time with Carnival Cruise Lines, I knew this run intimately so I was looking forward to San Juan especially as I had friends there, particularly Juan that owned the Small World bar.

I had been dealing for about an hour, when the manager approached me for a little chat.

"It always amuses me watching dice dealers deal blackjack"!

"I don't know what you are talking about, I don't deal dice"!

"What about roulette"?

"I don't deal that either, I deal blackjack and three card Caribbean stud poker"!

"Bollocks"!!!

"I beg your pardon"?

"You're telling me that you only deal BJ and 3 card CSP"?

"I am"!

157

"How the fuck did you get a job with this company then. Are you related to someone"?

"That's a bit harsh"!

"I, no sorry we need dice dealers and I thought you were coming on to help us out".

"Sorry about that but I can't help you".

I have to say that she was very nice about it just a little confused. We get to San Juan, and I explained to the casino crew I would show them the real Puerto Rico. I took them to a fantastic little restaurant that was cheap and to numerous bars that were the same. A great night was had by all.

We did Magen's Bay in St Thomas the next day, a truly beautiful beach on the north of the Island followed by drinks at Bruno's. I had dinner, went to work and then made a schoolboy error. Three days I had got away with it. No, I don't deal dice I said, never seen a dice table in me life I said, it all looks way too complicated for me I said. I had just dealt a seven-box losing hand on blackjack and proceeded to make the pay-outs in the only way that dice dealers know how. I didn't see the manager watching the game, so it came as no surprise when the whole pit heard the guvnor say, 'take that lying toe-rag off and send him to me'.

Captured!!!

With a great big smile on her face, she declared, "So, you are just a blackjack dealer"?

"I got away with it for three days".

"No, you never, I spoke to David last week and he informed me that you were at 'The Vic'. Quite excited he was"!

"Oh well it was good while it lasted".

"It's unusual, David"!

"What is"?

"Dice dealers wanting to deal blackjack".

"I have just dealt the game at 'The Vic' for two years solid. It is a very intense game as you know so I thought I would have some down time".

"That's all well and good, but can you go and sort that game out please as it is a fucking mess".

I genuinely wasn't prepared for what I was about to witness. I was stood behind the Boxman and watched as the stickman passed the next shooter the dice. In a very awkward fashion, he just about managed to manoeuvre the bones to the relevant guy and as the client picked up two dice out of five, the stick then leant all the way over to pick up the remaining three dice in a very strange position. He wasn't watching as the dice were thrown, because he was too busy trying to put the unused dice back in the bowl meaning there was an uneasy silence before the baseman called, 'six the point is six'. He marked the six whilst the Herbert down the other end marked the eight all the while the stickman's eyes are popping out of his head like a lizard on 'E'. The bets were coming in thick and fast but the baseman on the end where the dice were landing was putting the place bets on inside out (4 -10) rather than the other way round and the Boxman was not correcting them. He clearly didn't know. *Cue mayhem*. Punters at both ends were starting to voice their disapproval, 'what the fuck is going on here', was the general term used, so I took it upon myself to get on the stick and take charge of what was clearly a deteriorating position. Without anyone saying a word I tapped the stick out, got the dice back from whence they came and began to sort out the game.

"First and foremost, can you mark the proper number and put those bets from the six on the eight. You have got seventeen dollars on one bet and seven dollars on another so take a dollar off that bet and put it on that one so they should read six and eighteen, OK that's you sorted. Now to the other end, when you place bets, they are done the opposite way you have been doing them, and they are also paid the opposite way too, as in stick to base and not base to stick, but we will get to that later. Just do what I tell you, and everything will be OK". All said in a sedate calm voice that didn't antagonise anyone. The players were impressed, the management were particularly impressed, I was off to a good start. After about an hour or so the game died so I made a plea with the manager.

"Any danger I could go on blackjack".

"Come into my office Monza".

"How do you know my nickname"?

"You'll be surprised what I know about you"!

"Don't believe all the stories"!

"And I suppose that wanting to go and deal blackjack on that particular game has nothing to do with the blonde and brunette"?

"I didn't even notice them".

"Yeah, right"!

"I sorted the dice game out for you".

She motioned the pit-boss.

"Put him on there. This I must see"!

Once I was on that game, they didn't stand a fucking chance. It was a beautiful evening. The ocean was calm, the scene was set. There was an amazing red sky that seemed to penetrate through the water, there was a soft warm breeze and just a hint of calypso music in the background. It was perfect! I began critically thinking, the Boxman or supervisor as they were called did not have a clue as I made a couple of deliberate mistakes to see if he would correct me, but he didn't. Take in the fact there were two enormous ships being built at the same time and you can see why I thought I had made the right move.

"Hi".

It was the blonde and brunette.

"Ow r ya"?

"Man, we love the way you talk".

I don't know why, but American women dig our accent.

"What time are you done"?

"About midnight"!

"Shall we meet you in the club"?

"Sounds good".

They stood up, held hands and walked off with a cheerful bye in the air. I walked back into the casino to be met by the manager. Didn't take you long"!

"I don't know what you mean"?

"Anyway, don't get too comfortable".

"What"?

"You ain't gonna be on here that long".

"But I have only just got here"!

"I am not going to give you a big head Monza but you and I both know that you are not designed for this ship. You are going to be moved shortly, we need to find the cabin space that's all"!

"Any chance you know when"?

"Could be a week, could be six weeks but mark my words you are moving"!

This was a bit of a quandary, as I found myself in a somewhat strange position because I was the only one on board that knew the true mechanics of a dice game. How and when to take bets, how to place bets, how to announce bets so that everyone understood what the fuck was going on. Dice/craps is a very personal intense war of attrition that needs a running commentary. So, if you are of a nervous disposition or shy or don't like to communicate then jog-on as this is not the game for you. I couldn't give two fucks if you are the best pit dealer in the world, if you are not loud, comedic or for that matter downright arrogant then this is not for you. If you do not have the ability to take stick and more importantly give it, then again this is not for you. In my humble opinion one of the fundamental reasons that dice is dead in England, is because the people that elevate into management positions don't know the game, or don't know or like the clientele. It is unfathomable to me in an era when there are going to be a lot of casino closures in England, (and trust me they are coming) that dice is not the number one game. It is exciting, it is incomparable, it is a game that creates an environment of inclusion. From a punter's perspective it is a game of us against them. They scream, we deal, it is fun. If there are any casino directors out there that are looking for the next big thing, then you can do worse than put a dice table on your premises.

Friday and Saturday were sea days, so this gave me an opportunity to impart some of my knowledge. My strategy was to teach a method of dealing that would make it easier for us all, so we get through the shift with no drama, make some money by virtue of tips and get on with what we are there for. I am not Captain Fantastic; I was just trained correctly. The dice game in England is vastly different from the one in the States and in terms of what RCCL offered, it was light years away. RCCL ripped punters off. There existed a culture that was illegal, but they got away with it because there were no laws or governance at sea to police what the policy and procedure of the cruise line was. It was daylight/ocean going robbery that I personally found difficult to swallow.

In the first instance there was no come line. In the States, a fundamental strategy is a bet on the pass line with full odds followed by two come bets with full odds. In terms of a pass line bet the RCCL strategy was to discourage players taking their full odds behind the line, thereby creating an environment of negativity and distrust.

They created an impression they paid better odds on all the games. On dice all bets were for one and not to one, so a hard way bet that should be 7/1 or 9/1 was 8 or 10 for one. They could only take partial double odds behind the line but were highly discouraged from doing so. We didn't accept hopping bets and hard ways worked on the come-out, again - another strict no-no. However, the bugbear for me was the fact that we took bets on the pass line after a point had been established. This is a flagrant breach of the rules that I found utterly distasteful. It was the same with *put* bets. Instead of a come bet with full odds, you could place a bet straight in the number with odds without going through the come. So, a $10 put bet with full double odds with RCCL paid.

4&10 = $50
5&9 = $40
6&8 = $32

There was absolutely no need to create *put* bets, when you had *buy* bets and place bets which made much more sense. It was the same on blackjack, you got paid 6/5 instead of 6/4 for a two card twenty-one. It was replete throughout the casino on all the games but there was no point fighting it as all I saw was a company that was growing exponentially. I knew they would have to look at protocols as they were outdated. If they wanted to compete with other cruise lines and treated as an example of how a casino should function, they had to change. The players would demand it, or they would be subject to ridicule and in today's world of social media, they would have been destroyed.

There was also, the added bonus of taking dealers off if they started losing. If a dealer had shuffled what was an unlucky shoe for the house they were hauled off and abused. The same rules applied on roulette. If a dealer hit a couple of winning numbers, they were off to the sin bin. And my absolute favourite in all of this complete and utter bollocks was,

"Take that fucking canary off"!

"What canary? What are you talking about"?

"That ice-cream on stick, he's singing like a bird"!

In translation, this meant the stick, on dice had called three winners or conversely, the shooter had thrown three winners. Even though the stick, blackjack, roulette or Caribbean stud poker dealer had no influence on the outcome, according to the management, they were to blame, so they were castigated and subjected to dog's abuse.

Now let's look at the overall picture and, consider, not only did the casino shave the odds, but the management made it as difficult for the players to win as possible. I can't for the life of me understand how they tried to wring, every dollar out of the players when we had a captive audience. They couldn't go anywhere because they were on a ship! My belief was, we should have kept them entertained and given proper odds, more importantly, given them a fair deal, (if you'll excuse the pun)! As I am a firm believer, that rule number one in the hospitality business is, give the buyer/client/player something to develop a prosperous relationship. *If they like you, they will buy, if they don't, they won't!*

In the arena that was around at that time there was an horrendous atmosphere for real players because the casino management feared them. They didn't want them playing that's why the maximums were small, so the player didn't stand a chance of winning their money back if they got into trouble. They didn't play such was the petty mindedness.

9

There was nothing I could do at this stage as I was just a dealer but give me time and I'll develop my own strategy. One of fun, trust and professionalism. But for now, I just got on with it. There was no point talking to managers because they were paid a large percentage of both the slots and the tables, so I had to wait my turn in talking to the relevant powers that be.

I had two pit dealers for the afternoon, so I thought it prudent to start at the very beginning. Give them a chance to succeed. All people want is to be appreciated and recognised. Help them, and they won't forget you, do it properly and they will run through walls. It's a very simple exercise but uber effective. So, I showed them how to master the stick.

'The stick' on craps is responsible for the security of the dice. It is their responsibility to ensure they always have eyes on the di. To give a constant verbal running commentary of the action and act as a second pair of eyes for the Boxman. It is also their job to determine where and when the dice are thrown. To ensure that all crap eleven, centre, hopping and hard ways are paid and pressed, and the most important point in an aggressive game, keep the Boxman off your back.

Dice is not a game for the faint hearted, (not in England it ain't)! The game in the States is all about enjoyment, by being in Vegas and Atlantic City, you are in a resort, you have probably got a room for the weekend, and I am sure there are other flights of fancy that might tickle your wick. In England, the game was brutal. It was us against them. Fast, raw, loud, it was gambling at its best. The stick should be the first dealer they hear, so it is of paramount importance that you exude confidence. Look and sound like you know what you are doing and trust me the players will love you.

The stick itself is wooden, should be about four feet long with an L-shaped piece on the end that will enable you to manipulate and control the dice. It is flexible enough to bend into a horseshoe shape and should be considered an extension of your arm. A piece of kit that is irritating to get at first but once you have mastered, becomes an enjoyable experience. That's the easy part. Next, I explained how we determine who the next shooter is? An average dice table is roughly ten feet long and double ended. There is a baseman on both ends which is responsible for all pass line/don't pass line, come/don't come, no numbers, place/put/buy and field bets. It is also their role to take all centre action, whatever that may be and to ensure that the stick has placed, received and acknowledged the bet they are calling and vice versa. The stick is in the middle on the opposite side of the table, dictating the pace of the game as well as ensuring that all bets are recognised and paid correctly and the Boxman is the recorder of the team's deeds, the man that makes it all tick. *A royal pain in the arse!!!* The stick must sell the action, get the game moving and the player's involved but the Boxman is the guvnor, take my word for it.

Going from box to stick, the shooter is determined in a clockwise fashion. So, the player who is next to the baseman on the right-hand side, is the first to roll the dice. The conclusion of their hand is when a 'seven out' is rolled, meaning the player to their immediate left is the next shooter and so on.

I got both to understand that the stick won't snap, the players don't mind if you are loud (they really enjoy it actually), as it is an integral part of the experience and how to portray an image of enjoyment. I then showed them how to maintain control of the remaining dice that had not been thrown before we moved on to lesson two.

How to use the puck and mark the point. Again, a very simple but effective exercise. A baseman should pick up the puck with the inside hand to mark the point. There are a couple of crucial factors here. The first being it will leave your outside hand free to pay or take any winning or losing bets. Secondly and most importantly, it will give the Boxman a clear view of what you are doing. We ran this exercise until it became second nature. This was a good start. It gave them the confidence to go on a game and look like they knew what they were doing. If any Boxman had seen those procedures, they would have felt at ease.

Sunday was our home port and self-administration day. It was when you bought all your bits and when you made phone calls home etc. Fort Lauderdale is the number one destination for the college fraternity during spring break, it has an enormous sandy beach with bars, clubs and restaurants to match. It is an absolute dream for young people as it caters for their every whim. If I was of a younger disposition and had an opportunity to pick a destination anywhere on the globe that I could holiday, then Fort Lauderdale would be it. There is even a word for it in the dictionary, (*fantastic*)!

I threw myself at Lauderdale with gusto. Breakfast at Denny's followed by a couple of hours shopping, then down to Las Olas for a dip, finished off with lunch at any number of archetypal good American diners. I could never get enough of a good burger with fries and onion rings in the States.

10

The start of a cruise was a venture for vultures. A similar scenario to a version of circling the wagons. All the petty officers were on parade as proud as punch displaying their blue stripes. It was always fun to watch so called *officers,* who were food and beverage Herbert's pretending to be someone. It was hilarious watching them flutter around the ladies only to fail spectacularly!

Note to Herbert's.

Once a Herbert, always a Herbert and no amount of little blue stripes are going to earn you a bunk-up!

We in the casino department however were the epitome of cool. If you were on the early shift, you were in black and whites ready to start work in about half an hour. I can't speak for anyone else, but I always felt extremely comfortable in a Tuxedo, crisp white shirt, pukka pair of cufflinks and an undone bow tie hanging from your shirt. If you were on the late shift you were dressed in uber-cool, trendy beach ready Floridian attire, complete with an ice-cold beer. It was a dress rehearsal for the forthcoming week's shenanigans, an opportunity to eye up the talent. Personally, I used it as an exercise by way of an introduction to being English. I would walk to the bar and order in my loudest cockney accent, any libation that took my fancy. For example, "Four bottles of Corona, please"?

"Oh man, are you from England"?

"Yes, love"! We're off and running.

The weight of a casino's cruise business can be judged by the amount of passenger's attendance at the tables in the first hour of the cruise. Gamblers are like that. Not for them is the old, 'let's have a couple of drinks with dinner before we start malarkey'. They are itching to play from the off. The unfortunate thing for us on the Azure was any real players were on 'The Sov', meaning we were generally quiet.

However, what The Azure lacked in readies, it more than made up for in fun. Because of its lack of size, it was a much more intimate affair whereby everyone knew everybody.

It was a relatively quiet night, so I got an early chop. For anyone that missed the Sail away party the catch up was the first night at the club. A very small tastefully done facility that was ripe for making acquaintances. Scott and I surveyed our domain, ordered a couple of drinks, then ……….

"There are a lot of good-looking Richard's on this week"

"Yes, mate, there are"!

"Shall we"?

"Fucking right we will"!

There is only ever going to be one winner out of, nightclub or cabin party. A cabin party will win every single time. It was never open to debate and if you ask any passengers that made the party, they will tell you it was the best time they had all week. Rule No.1 on a cruise ship, 'what goes on in a cabin party, stays in a cabin party'. There is a multitude of words you could use to describe them but because they were, shall we say, adult in nature, I would say they were immense. It was our chance to let loose, let our hair down so to speak, to have a go at the morons that ask stupid questions.

"What time is the midnight buffet"?

I first heard that question more than thirty years ago. It beggar's belief at the level of stupidity that some passengers revert to. I would just look at them with utter contempt. 'Are you a fucking idiot"? No, I never said that, but I wanted to. A typical response would go something like this,

"I'm 100% certain that midnight in the States is the same as it is in Europe".

"Yes, it is".

Then I would walk off and leave them to their own devices. There was this uncomfortable silence as the realisation of the moronic question they asked sank in. However, the king of kings, the dumbest question I got asked was at the photo gallery one evening. I had popped down to see my pal who was working the till to ask if he fancied a light ale. He was transfixed on a client that looked confused, so during their dilemma, he went over to offer his services.

"Hello mate, may I help you"?

"Yes, you can"!

In as loud a voice and as proud as punch, he said, *"How do I know which pictures mine"?*

What a fucking imbecile! If you know anybody that has ever asked that question, then you have my unreserved permission to shoot them in the face. You must be the biggest fucking dick in the history of mankind. I defy anyone that lives on Planet Earth to send me a dumber question than that. I wholeheartedly guarantee that there is not an individual on this spherical orb we call home, that has ever posed as stupid a question as that.

We were about half an hour in now, and the party was swinging. Shop assistants, photographers, cruise staff (child molesters), entertainers, dancers, casino crew, even a couple of officers. Word had got out that there was a new man in town and boy did I milk it!

House music was the thing at the time, and I had half a dozen up to the minute, properly mixed, fresh off the press cassette tapes. The cabin was absolutely rocking to the beat of Italian House. Dancers were dancing, singers were singing and the casino crew, well they were just at it. I was properly giving it some now, a shoeshine shuffle of immense proportions when I got accosted by a lithe dancer from New York.

She held out her hand and led me straight to her room. She didn't give a fuck that her roommate was lying there with her earphones on listening to her Walkman. Ploughed straight into me for all she was worth.

Labadee (Haiti)

RCCL had unprecedented access to a cut off beach in Haiti named Labadee. It was their own private island if you like. About a mile long sandy beach with shrubbery and hammocks at the back, it was a perfect way to relax and plan your next stop, San Juan. There is not a lot to relate about Labadee as it was a beach that we went by charter as even The Azure was too big to dock. A little bit of snorkelling would be about as exciting as it could get. So, after a dip, it was back for an evening's work and the promise of waking up in the morning to…

San Juan (Puerto Rico)

There are not enough superlatives in the dictionary to describe San Juan. An old Spanish domicile it was as dangerous as fuck. It was in the air, in the streets, it enveloped your every being.

Don't stray from the official tours. Don't get into unlicensed cabs. Be vigilant after dark in Old San Juan. Be careful of drug dealers. Shouldn't have told me that. It was a red flag to a bull. Why go there in the first place. Yes, you had to be careful but there are places in cities all over England where you have to watch yourself. Once you had taken your balls out of the bedside cabinet, you can rest assured that San Juan was fantastic. I always done a recce of my locality and SJ was no different. Of course, I went to where you were not supposed to, it made it exciting, and I couldn't give two fucks anyway.

An old town that had a terrific underbelly of youth culture and dance, was constantly throbbing to the beat of House Music. It was the early nineties; I was twenty-nine and physically in the shape of my life. Armed with a couple of brand spanking freshly mixed House Music tapes, I decided to go in search of what SJ had to offer. So, complete with the biggest sombrero in the world I went shopping.

My previous experience of Old San Juan was of the night-time economy because when I worked for Carnival, the Celebration never docked until 5 pm. Now we were there at 10 am it created a whole new world of opportunity. Not for me was a trip to the rainforest, I am a council estate kid. I like bricks and mortar, noise, loud music and lots of people. It was about midday, so the streets were aplenty with American tourists getting ripped the fuck off by savvy Puerto Ricans. I was mooching when a familiar sound hit me. It was a 'Balou' the bear moment, you know where he is staking out Mowgli and he hears the beat. Then he starts dancing and declares something like, 'I'm gone man, solid gone'. I managed to find a record shop that sold the latest vinyl from New York and Chicago. In a deep East coast accent, the guy behind the counter says, "That's a big fucking hat"!

He was talking about my rather uncouth sombrero, which I thought was apt considering it was about a million degrees in the SJ heat.

"I've only been here a couple of weeks so I'm just getting used to the heat".

"Yeah, man, whatever".

"Take it or leave mate, anyway, do you have a track by"? *whomever the artist was at the time knowing he wouldn't have it!*

"What sort of genre is that"?

"House".

"Hey, man, are you from England"?

"Yes, I am".

"You got anything with you"?

"Just so happens I do"!

I produced the two tapes out of my pocket.

"Ow bout this. I'll leave you the tapes and come back later".

"You trust me, man"?

"Hundred per cent".

"OK brother we shut at nine".

Got him. I knew he would love these tapes. No let me re-phrase that. He was *gonna* do cartwheels!

I ventured into the heat to find a coffee shop and sat outside underneath a parasol with a pizza and an iced coffee, when I was disturbed by the dancer from New York.

"Hi".

"Hello, you"!

"I've been looking for you".

This was not good. I had no problem with our little dalliances, but I certainly did not want a relationship. I was perturbed!

"What's up"?

"I have something to tell you".

Not even my little soldiers work that quickly -

"I'm going home".

"That's great".

"I thought you would be upset".

"What"?

"Well, you know".

Exchanging body fluids over two days a relationship does not make, so I explained it to her.

"I don't know about you, but I have enjoyed our little time together"

"I was falling for you".

"After two fucking days. Don't be so ridiculous!!! Think of New York".

"It's my last night in San Juan. Wanna spend it with me"?

"Absofuckinglutely"!

There are worst ways to spend an afternoon. We went to a local public beach and had a day, similar to that of any couple that frolicked in the Caribbean. We had an early evening meal with a couple of cocktails followed by a trip to the record shop. Soon as we walked in my date let out a shriek.

"What the fuck".

The guy behind the counter had a great big grin on his face.

"How you doing"?

"I've been coming here for six months, and I never knew you were in town."

"Left the shop on Christopher and Bleeker and decided to come home".

"You look good".

"So do you".

After a love in and what seemed like a mutual appreciation society, we moved on.

"Sorry to interrupt you but did you like the tapes"?

"This is sick shit man; you have to come and play at my club"!

"Sorry"?

"You mixed this right"?

"No mate, a pal of mine done 'em"!

"He's good, music too"!

With my newfound respect from the chaps of Puerto Rico, my date and I made our way back to the ship to freshen up and a promise that we would meet the guys for drinks at the Small World bar in San Juan at nine. We had about an hour to spare so as you can imagine I was thinking of something sinful, as you do in the presence of such company when the dancer noticed something.

"Have you seen this"?

"Seen what"?

"This"!

We were in reception at the purser's desk when she pulled up a leaflet that was aimed at the crew but had managed to find its way into the excursion tray. In big bold letters it read,

Monza On the March

For a Puerto Rico experience like no other,

Join Monza and crew for fun in the sun.
8:30 at the Purser desk

It would seem the word had spread amongst the crew that the previous week's shenanigans had caused something of a stir. Without telling me, they produced this piece of paperwork secure in the knowledge I would go along with it. As I left my cabin there was a feeling of expectancy, something in the air. I climb the two flights of stairs to be greeted by a cheer. With everyone a little tanked and excited, we attacked Old San Juan.

"To boldly go where no man has gone before"

As we passed the Small World bar some of the crew started to get a little excited because we were now into forbidden territories. Our first port of call was a little bar on Calle San Jose. It had a bar with about four stools on the right, a pool table out the back and a cassette deck. I put a tape on and got to work. Within half an hour and a couple of drinks the party was in full swing. The atmosphere was insane, I showed them a side of San Juan they hadn't experienced before, where they had been told to avoid. We venture further, deeper into the realms where the locals go for entertainment. We find another bar that had a DJ spinning the latest Puerto Rican House. Right on cue Kelly and the boys appear.

'*Avin it*' would be a phrase synonymous with the evening as everyone around was smiling, laughing, dancing. We went to a couple more establishments they had not been to before the customary charge back to the ship, and the 1:30 am curfew.

This was when the fun really started as we were berthed in a passenger area. There must have been at least half a dozen cabins that had parties in full flow, the ship was absolutely rocking, literally. The first cabin to come out and complain were an elderly pair from New York. Within five minutes and having had a conversation with Kelly, the old girl sidles up to me, 'you got any blow'? Having a loud party in passenger areas is one thing, having a party and supplying cocaine to passengers is quite another! I respectfully declined but what happened next made me chuckle, "Come with me oldie"! says Kelly, holding out her hand with a great big grin on her face!

They re-surfaced about twenty minutes later howling laughing. I am not one to judge, particularly when it comes to ageism, but I would hazard a guess and say with hand on heart I bet this lady was a right hoot when she was younger.

"Oh, David you have made an old lady extremely happy"!

She slides in next to me, raises an eyebrow, and proceeds to stroke the inside of my leg. I sat there frozen, then she starts giggling like a child, lets out a shriek and walks off never to be seen again. *You couldn't make it up*, but I bet the old boy she was with had a night to remember.

The casino was relatively busy considering the first two days. I was on the dice table with the two guy's that I had spent a little time training when a nice little hand started developing. The ice-cream that was the suit comes over and tries to put a new set of dice in my hands.

"What the fuck are you doing"?

"Change the dice"!

"What"?

"Because the canary over there is singing like a bird"!

"Have you lost your mind"?

"I mean it, change the dice"!

Let battle commence.

"You change the dice, you fucking moron"!

He looked at me totally shocked. I was staring at him like the cretin he was.

"How the fuck, is changing the dice going to influence the outcome of the next decision"?

"And take him off the stick as well"!

"You fucking take him off"!

I wasn't having it. This had nothing to do with the fact I had no respect for him as he had blagged a suit's job by virtue of his so-called dice experience. I felt that what he wanted to do was wrong, at every level it was wrong! I was in the middle of the pit now, glaring at him in a very aggressive stance. I was ready to '*chin-im*' there and then, so I said matter of factly, "You are a fucking imbecile! I know it, we all fucking know it, now *jog-on!*

I went back to the dice table fuming. The boys stood still not knowing what to do, the punters were staring at me. In a very calm voice I stated, "Shall we"?

The game had stopped to watch the little spectacle. I had clearly got the better of this exchange, but I knew this would not be the end of it. It was only just beginning.

"Move the dice guys, let's go"!

With a knowing wink from the shooter and a feeling of contentment from within the crew we get the game going. About nine o'clock when the game had died. I looked at the stick whose face had gone a funny colour. The tap on my shoulder told me it was time for round two. It was the manager.

"Can you come with me please Monza"?

Without a word of acknowledgement, I winked at the crew, stood up and followed her to a little room behind the bar.

"Before I start do you have anything to say".

I stood there ready to absorb the onslaught safe in the knowledge this was a discussion she could not win.

"Did you tell a supervisor to fuck off"?

"No, I told him to jog-on"!

"That's the same thing"!

"Semantics"!

"Anyway, it is company policy to change the dice if they are unlucky".

"Define unlucky".

"If a player shoots too many winners".

"What about if he was playing on the miss"?

"I don't know what you mean"!

"Exactly, you don't know what I mean and more importantly you don't know what you are talking about"!

"I beg your pardon"?

"You heard. Can I have it writing"?

"Can you have what in writing"?

"That a global cruise line like RCCL have a policy in their casino department that if a player on craps shoots three or more winners, they change the *unlucky* dice"!

"Don't be so ridiculous"!

"Why not, that is your current position"

I don't know whether she developed a rush of blood or whether she was just extremely embarrassed, but she went a tad red. I pressed on.

"Why on Earth would you do such a thing"?

"It is something we have always done"

"I ain't doing it and you can take it from me that I won't let anyone commit that sort of bollocks. Not while I'm here. Not on my table"!

She knew I was right. There is no logical explanation for that kind of behaviour. It is beyond the realms of common sense. I refer to a statement I mentioned earlier. There is no such thing as luck from a dealer's perspective. It doesn't exist. There is not a dealer in the world who can spin a specific number or deal a certain hand from a shuffled shoe. Consequently, there is not a stickman who can manipulate or predict an outcome on the next roll of the dice because he/she has no control of two dice thrown ten feet in the air.

The door opened and I came out before the manager. I had a look of pure professionalism whilst my colleague had a face like a slapped arse. The whole casino crew were looking, waiting for any sign of conflict. But they didn't get one. It was not my objective to win a battle, I saw it as an opportunity to try and make the manager see sense. Whom ever had started this procedure had a case to answer in my book? To change the dice and the stick because the shooter has thrown a few winners is beyond idiotic. Reluctantly and I mean very reluctantly she agreed. Because she was institutionalised, she had failed to see the wood through the trees. The fantastic money she was earning had left her bereft of any balance. It was just plain wrong.

We move on.

We closed the casino, and I went straight to bed, I never had a shower or brushed my teeth, I just got undressed and fell into a deep contented sleep. I had lunch in the mess, got ready for work, when suddenly it dawned on me that they hadn't seen me perform properly yet. I had been full of this and that, so it was about time that I unleashed the full force of how a dealer from 'The Vic' does it. As luck would have it, I get to work, and the crew are putting the float out and about six or seven players are waiting for it to open.

I walked to the cash desk, sign the dice out and bounced over to the table. The energy was evident. I was ready, the players were ready, the crew were eager to see if I was all mouth and trousers. If they were, they were disappointed as from the moment that I unwrapped the six di and put them on the table it was clear who was-in-charge of this little scenario. I presented the first shooter with the di who picked two leaving me to retrieve the remaining four and place them in the bowl.

"OK shoots, seven eleven you win, let's go"!

For the next hour I ran the game to the best of my ability. I stayed on the stick for a couple of reasons. The first was to prove a point. What and when to call, the volume, pitch and commentary. Basically, to maintain a level of control that was conducive to an environment of fun and professionalism. In my opinion it was how every dice game should be run. Secondly it gave me an opportunity to assess the level and quality of the rest of the crew. Apart from Scott Rudd, I had a bit of work on my hands, but we could and would work on that. I spent the next day as a professional. Before the close of play on the last day I was approached by the manager.

"I have to say David I'm impressed".

"Thank you".

"You are a little arrogant but then all dice dealers are"!

"Yes, I'm arrogant, confident and assertive, the game demands it".

"If you say so. Anyway, I am going to speak with David about you tomorrow".

"Sweet".

"See you tomorrow".

It was the end of my second week and all-in-all it was a good start. I had developed a sound footing of good professional relationships, had some fun with the ladies and the coup-de-grace, we were in Fort Lauderdale tomorrow. I went straight to bed to ensure that I would get up early so I could enjoy what the fruits of the mid-east coast of Florida had to offer. *I was never disappointed!*

The next three or four weeks were much the same. The dice crew were coming along nicely, I was settled in, and **Monza on The March** had reached legendary status. So much so that during one of the welcome aboard speeches by the cruise director and what to expect for the next week from your cruise, my little excursion got a mention. Something along the lines of what time the shops open, the casino, the spa, what to expect in Labadee,

San Juan, and those of you who like a night out with drinks, fun, and a little boogie then maybe **MOTM** may tickle your fancy! *Boom I was infamous!*

I was amid my sixth cruise, had just completed a tour of **MOTM** when I was approached by the casino manager in the nightclub.

"I want a word with you"!

Not good!

"What have I done"?

"Nothing, you're getting off in Lauderdale".

"Why"?

"You're going on the Sovereign. You have two days in the Miami Marriott on Bayshore Drive, then fly to Puerto Rico and join the ship Tuesday"

To say I was excited would have been an understatement. I flung myself at the nightclub to tell everybody. We had a cabin party to remember, a last hurrah on the soon to be defunct Azure Seas and me with a future of the best seven months of my life to look forward to.

11

Like a bowling ball through the port, I joined the line of two at the taxi rank for all-of about thirty seconds, dumped my bags in the boot and declared,

"Miami".

"Where to man"?

"The Marriott, Bayshore Drive, Biscayne Bay"!

"That's about a hundred bucks"!

"I don't give a fuck"!

I like Fort Lauderdale, but it's not Miami. I was absolutely buzzing. It was only 8 am, but I was like a cat on a hot tin roof.

Approximately forty-five minutes and sixty-five bucks later, we pull up outside the Marriott, home to Tugboat Annie's. At 9 am Sunday morning, I call the airline to re-arrange my ticket, so I could sample what San Juan had to offer over three days. It worked. They pushed my flight forward to today at 3 pm. I left my bags in the hotel luggage hold and got a taxi to the beach to have breakfast at the News Cafe.

9:30 am on a Sunday is early for South Beach. Even though it was mid-morning, I had enough time to have a light bite before a casual walk along the beach in preparation for an afternoon flight then an evening with Juan at the Small World bar in Puerto Rico.

The flight was smooth. I got a taxi to the Caribe Hilton, about ten minutes from the cruise terminal. Booked in and fired up, I made my way over to Old San Juan to see Juan. As I entered, it took him a few moments to realise who I was, but once the initial shock was gone. He muttered something in Spanish, locked the bar and out we went into the undeniably funky Puerto Rican air.

No matter how much you think you know somewhere, you will never know it like a local. I am immensely proud of coming from West London, I am a segment of the produce of that part of London. I understand the mechanics of how it works, the makeup of the people. I have a deep understanding of the mindset and mentality of that part of society. It is who I am. So as Juan and I push deeper into the realms of an environment I am unfamiliar with, I found it best to let him take the lead.

We were at the north side walking along Calle Norzagaray, did a sharp left into Calle Bajada Matadero and into an area that had one of the highest murder rates per capita in the world (outside of a war zone) at the time. It was familiar territory to me as this was where I used to get my sniff from. Under the bridge and about one hundred yards ahead was painted a thick white line on the road, which was an indicator for the next dealer to pick up his fishing tackle box and furnish you with your class 'A'. It was also their way of telling you, not to go any further as they considered that insulting. This was their turf, their little piece of Puerto Rico. It was an exercise in hilarity, standing in line trying to avoid eye contact with anyone as we all worked on various cruise lines, but there was something exciting about it too. Unbeknownst to us at the time, it was also one of the safest places to go because the dealers needed our dollar, so they ensured everyone's safety, albeit we were unaware. Anyway, Juan and I walk over the line and into a bar across the road when he laughs,

"I bet you never thought you would be drinking in this bar".

"No, I didn't"

He orders a bottle of tequila, and we settle into a corner plot with a couple of the locals. About an hour or so later, I've got tequila, cerveza and a whisky on the go when one of Juan's lady friends sits on my lap and starts whispering sweet nothing's in my ear. *In Spanish!* I didn't have a clue what she was saying because it looked for all the world that she was propositioning me. So, I look at Juan for some help, but he's rolling around in hysterics, whilst at the same time gesturing for me to go with her as we were going to someone's place to carry on the party.

"I know what you are thinking, David, but we are going to my sister's place for a fiesta, and you are invited"!

"Sweet"

"It will be, just wait until we get there"!

My imagination began to run wild; I mean, what the fuck was I thinking. I come from a tough corner of London, but this was a different kettle of fish. This was proper *big boy shit*. Together through the streets of the unknown, we finally arrive. 'Ola David' cried the welcoming crowd. A bottle of Corona and a half-cut straw is thrust in my hand with a gesture to help myself to a line of the mountain that was on the table three steps to my left. 'Don't mind if I do', I thought. The lady that held my hand all the way to the party then comes over and wants a dance. We were getting very familiar with each other when suddenly, I got a tap on my shoulder from Juan asking me to go with him into a little room at the side of the house. As I enter, it was abundantly clear that I was here for something serious, the two gentlemen that were in attendance were obviously here to discuss a potential business proposition, and I knew exactly what they wanted before it even came out of their mouths.

Juan and the two guys start to engage in Spanish. It was all light-hearted before one of them looked at me, and the dynamic of the conversation took a different course. You don't need to speak another language to understand when things turn nasty, so I decided to interject. In as crisp a New York accent as you can imagine, the taller one of the two says,

"I'm a cousin of Kelly".

"The dancer"?

"Yes"!

"And"

"She says you fucked her about"!

"No I never, we had a couple of nights together!"

The two boys get into a fierce exchange, gesticulating as only Latin's do. They pretty much got into a shoving match when Juan intervened. The silence that ensued seemed to go on for ages before finally, they all broke into a fit of giggling. Juan spoke first,

"David, these are my two nephews, and your dancer friend Kelly (which isn't her real name) is my niece. They are just a little protective, that's all. Unfortunately, you are the latest in a long line of guys she falls for in rapid time. It's what she does"!

The two boys are smiling now. One of them pulls a bag out of his pocket and gestures for me to hold my hand out. I make a fist, and he pours a little pocket of yayo onto the back of it, which I hoover up in a second. (God, this gear is strong!) As they were about to start, I said in a firm voice,

"No"!

"You don't know what we are going to ask"!

"Do you think I came down the Thames on a fucking bicycle? I haven't been on the ship yet. I don't know the layout. I don't know the security detail. I don't know the crew. I've not even seen the fucking thing"!

After about ten seconds of silence, one of my newly acquired Puerto Rican/New York buddies' states,

"He's our guy"!

"Told you so"! says Juan.

Now it was my turn.

"Before anyone starts counting their chickens and you start formulating a strategic plan to export your product, there is a lot of reconnaissance ahead of us"!

"How long"?

"At least a month".

"Sounds about right".

"What sort of weight are we talking"?

"As much as you can handle".

"Thought you were going to say that".

The boys were a part of a much wider network but just wanted to make a little extra on the side. In other words, they were being greedy!

"I'll have a look and let you know soon as"

"OK cool"

With a wink from Juan, it was time to get down and dirty. We stepped back into the party and had a blast until mid-afternoon Monday. I had had enough at this point, so it was a quick ride back to the Caribe Hilton and sleep. I went to bed contented and dreamt of my immediate future and what the Sovereign would hold in store. I would be far from disappointed.

I managed to get a good night's kip, had a hearty breakfast, then had an hour or so on the beach in preparation for my stint on a new ship. On approach to the cruise terminal, you are immediately struck by the sheer enormity of Sovereign of The Seas. You can't miss her! Being the biggest, grandest ship in the world at seventy-five thousand tonnes, she was the result of modern engineering at its finest. A football pitch long and carrying two thousand eight hundred and fifty passengers and almost nine hundred and fifty crew, she sailed seven-day cruises in the Caribbean all year round.

I was the sole employee signing on that day, so after about ten minutes, I was shown to my cabin. In terms of room space, they were about half the size of the cabins on the Azure, but that never bothered me as I always treated them as somewhere to sleep. As far as I was concerned, they were for washing, sleeping and shagging in any order you prefer. Even though we were living and working on board, I never felt it was home. Unpacked and dressed in beach attire, I got a cab to playa el escambron for the afternoon before yet another evening in Old San Juan.

On return from the beach, I made my way to my cabin and what struck me was the feeling of a party. Nearly all the cabin doors were open with various tastes in music playing. It was about 7 pm, so the crew were getting ready for the evening when one of the guys came up to me and made an introduction,

"Alo mate".

"Alright".

"You the new guy"?

"I am"!

"I'm Justin. You coming out"?

"I'm David, why not"?

"Get dressed, and I'll show you San Juan"!

If only he knew, I didn't have the heart to tell him. Anyway, I thought I'd start slowly.

"What time"?

"Whenever you're ready".

"Sweet, give me ten minutes".

Big J and I headed for the Small World bar.

"You ever been to San Juan before David"?

"Once or twice"!

"I've got to meet a couple of birds in the Small World bar. Fancy one in there"?

"I'll give it a try".

I saw Juan's niece at the bar. I didn't see Justin trying to make introductions as I went straight over to Juan and company. I only left them a day earlier, but you would have thought it was years, anyway, Juan poured drinks for us, then I went over to Justin and friends to offer them a drink. On cue, the barman produces a bottle of tequila, some glasses and four bottles of Mexican beer. Juan comes over and says if anyone is a friend of mine, they are a friend of his. If we need any more drinks, let him know as it will be on the house. Suitably impressed, Justin's girlfriend introduces herself,

"Hi, I'm Elnima".

"David".

Justin butts in,

"Hold on a minute. You're not Monza are you"?

"I am"!

"Fucking hell! I have heard a lot about you".

"Don't believe all the stories".

"What about some of them"?

"I'll let you make your own mind up"!

I was attracted to Elnima. Head over heels in lust. She was right up my street, a dancer, vivacious, beautiful with a propensity to entertain. If there was anyone that was born to be on the stage, it was her. I was struck.

Bollocks, what the fuck do I do now? I know, I'll ignore her, try to avoid her, after all we are on the biggest cruise ship in the world. We were in St Thomas the next day, and I thought it would be prudent to go to a beach on my own and collect my thoughts. Instead of going to Magen's Bay which was the overwhelming choice of the masses, I went to Lime Tree Beach the best-kept secret in St Thomas. Unfortunately for me, she was there with two of her friends in a bikini. *In a fucking bikini!* I got through the day, and it was time to start my career as a dealer on board 'The Sov'.

I make my way to the casino to be met by the manager,

"You're the dice dealer".

"Something like that".

"I don't have time to talk now, David, so let's do it later"!

"OK".

"Go on dice please, there's quite a game on there".

Ten minutes later, I got tapped out, put my jacket on and went to watch the show. It was her again. Lead dancer she was. I couldn't take my eyes off her. She had an incredible body, rhythmic, lithe and athletic. She absolutely owned that stage. Man, I was hooked. I was on fire, so on my return to the table, I sneaked on the sausage roll (pole/stick), and before anyone had a chance to protest, I gave the shooter the dice. As he throws them, there is a collective 'No', too late.

"Seven out, line in the don't sides win, last come gets some, pay the bets behind"!

The two basemen and Mark (Ranf) Ranford just looked at me, utterly beaten. They never said a word. I laid the stick on the table and said,

"Don't ever push the dice on me again, you ain't fucking quick enough"!

Point very much proven, I march over to the pit when Ranf calls me back,

"Fair enough, Monz. I'm Ranf. Can you go back on the stick, please"!

"Certainly".

Introductions made we end the dick-swinging competition and get on with the job at hand. I was lucky that night as I got an early chop, so it was off to the disco for a taste of the nightlife. I get to the bar, and there she is again. I can't help myself,

"Would you like a drink"

"I'll have whatever you're having"!

"Two bottles of Corona, please, barman"!

"Coming right up"!

With the drinks ordered, I looked at her, not saying a word. She looked at me in stone-cold silence. I looked at her face, the outline of her physique, her hair and then deep into her eyes, it was reciprocated. The drinks came, I tipped my bottle to her, said cheers and then,

"Take care".

"Night-Night David"!

We never took our eyes off each other. You would have had to have been deaf, dumb and fucking blind not to have felt the energy and sexual tension. However, she was with another guy, so that was that. I got through the next two days like a stroll in the park. After we finished on Friday, the manager called me over.

"Ranf has given you a glowing report".

"Thanks"

"If you carry on like this, I think we both know where this is going"!

"I hope so"!

"Well, it's a good start".

I went to bed content in the knowledge that there was a lot of scope for promotion within the company, the Monarch and the Majesty both sister ships of 'The Sov' were debuting the early part of next year. It was time to get my head down.

12

In the of the Port of Miami is a Seaman's Centre that used to cater for the guy's and girls that worked the ships. It had a cafe, swimming pool, any number of phone booths for people to maintain relationships with their loved ones at home, and the coup-de-grace, was a football pitch that ran a league. It was organised by an administrator attached to the centre as they supplied the kit, boots and referee. It was a basic but effective set-up. I had already been to Flagler to pick up me bits, dropped them off at the ship, checked my watch, and it was still before mid-day. I haven't spoken to Nan for a while, so I'll give her a call. It would lift morale. Enroute, I don't know whether you call this timing, luck or divine intervention, a waiter that worked on 'The Sov' asked if I fancied a game of football? He caught me at exactly the right time, I was dying for a game of football.

I played my first game for 'The Sov'. It went surprisingly well with me scoring four goals in a six-nil win. I didn't bother waiting to get in the changing room to shower; I just took my boots off and dived in the pool, *fucking lovely it was!* I got a burger and fries, booked a booth and gave Esther Power a call.

Encouraged and heartened, I was just about to go on a table when an announcement was made over the tannoid system.

"David Moynihan from the casino department to the hotel manager's office. Immediately"!

The manager came striding over,

"What the fuck"!

"Ain't got a Danny".

"You been up to something Monz"?

"I don't think so".

"Well, you had better go and see what he wants".

I promise you I was in the dark as much as anyone, but I had a bit of a Blaise attitude because, as far as I was aware, I hadn't broken any rules. All the casino crew were looking at me like I was about to walk a gangplank and certain death. With a twinkle in my eye, I went to see what the big boss had to say for himself.

"You asked to see me"?

"Hi David, I'm Lars. Come in".

I have to say he was very welcoming.

"A little birdie tells me you play football".

"Everyone I know plays football".

"To the same level as you".

"In most cases, a lot better"!

"OK, I'm not interested in them; I am a self-confessed football nut. I want to win the cruise ship league, and I want you to help me do it".

"I'll need access to all the various departments on Saturdays".

"Done".

"I'll need to have a trial game in San Juan on Tuesday to look for any prospective players".

"I'll action that including transport to and from the pitch".

"You will need to make an announcement that I would like to have a meeting at one o'clock tomorrow regarding the football team in the crew bar"!

"I'll make sure that all the relevant parties are aware that we are going to take this seriously"!

"Sounds good"

"So, you will be the coach? Do we have a deal"?

He held out his hand, which I shook vigorously.

"OK, David, anything you need, do not hesitate to come and see me".

"Will do"

I walked into the pit and the craziest dice game I ever came across at sea. Ranf the Boxman asks,

"Was he alright"?

"Sweet, he wants me to coach the football team".

"Let's sort this out first, and then we'll discuss it over a light ale later"!

I had kept to myself for all-of about three days, but by virtue of my new coaching position, I was going to put myself about a bit. So gone was the reserved and polite David, and in came the lairy know-it-all, best stickman in the world, Monza! I wasted no time in approaching the sweaty socks on the firm. Two Glaswegians, Andy Mcgowan, Tony Minchello and the outsider from Dundee, Paul Chiver's otherwise known as McGoo, Chin-

Chin and PC who were dubbed the *'Sweaty Mafia'*. All of them fine footballers agreed to be a part of 'The Sov' football project.

Next to be approached were two good players in the photographer department, Andy and Nick, who again agreed on the spot, it was a good start, but because of time restraints, the rest would have to wait until tomorrow's meeting.

Saturday night in the club was a strong indicator of who the party animals were. Not for them was the mantra, 'early to bed, early to rise' rather 'let's have a lite-ale, a line of Charlie and we'll worry about tomorrow when that comes'. These were my kind of people. If there is one thing about Americans that I love, it is the *'work hard, play hard'* philosophy they exude. I was done about one, so I thought I would pop my head in the door and have a look. *She* was in there looking fabulous as usual. It was doing my head in, so I thought I'd have one drink and an early night. Then completely out of the blue, she came over,

"Would you like a drink"?

"No thanks, love, I'm only having the one".

"Are you sure? I'm buying"!

"Listen 'ere girl, there's something I have-to get off my chest. I'm not standing here looking at you in that fucking dress. I have some serious impure thoughts going on in my head, and quite frankly, I want on the firm, but as you are with someone else it's doing my nut in"!

"What are you talking about"?

"Your boyfriend"!

"What boyfriend"?

"But I thought".

"Well, you thought wrong. Now, what about that drink"?

I don't do chat-up-lines, but that was how it started. Simple as that. If there was any doubt in my mind about relationship's, they were quickly dispelled as I fell head over heels in love with her from the off. I was captivated, conquered even, she had me hook, line and sinker, from the very beginning, but more of that later, it was time to get to work.

I had a meeting with prospective footballers at one o'clock in the crew bar. There were approximately forty guy's that fancied their chances, so I laid out some guidelines. You had to be available every Saturday, or you couldn't play. This was difficult as in some departments this time was crucial, as cabin stewards and waiters, had to meet their clients by way of an introduction. I stressed the point that nepotism and favouritism were excluded as if they showed the right attitude - you were in, if you didn't, you were out. No exceptions. There was a trial game on Tuesday in San Juan so, anybody that wanted to be in the side had to attend, and I would let the players know after that. As a unit, there was a very positive response, so I grabbed a spot of lunch and made my way to work.

We were lucky in the casino department as we only opened in international waters. On a sea day, we got going at two so, enroute to work dressed in my tuxedo, crisp white shirt, pukka cufflinks and bowtie, complete with a name badge the size of Alaska, I get accosted in the atrium by yet another Herbert,

"Hey man, do you work on the ship"?

"No mate, I'm taking my tuxedo for a swim, you absolute pillock!"

"Whaaaaat"?

There is no point answering because they don't understand us. So, I stood there and stared at him.

"What time is the midnight buffet"?

Before I gave my response there are several things to consider, firstly they had just finished lunch because they were coming out of the restaurant. Secondly, he's not going to understand me as he will look at his missus and say, "What'd he say"? Thirdly he is a cretin, and he is not worthy of any more of my valuable time. So, I walked off, leaving him somewhat bemused.

Note to future cruisers. If someone is dressed in a tuxedo at two in the afternoon with a name badge on, you can rest assured they work on the ship. Come to think of it, I may as well clarify a few more points whilst we are at it. The no. 1 rule in all of this.

You do not leave your brain at the Purser's desk when you embark!!!

Here are the answers to a few of your idiotic questions:

1. *"What time is the midnight Buffet"?*

Answer. **Midnight!**

2. *"Do these stairs go up"?*

Answer. **You are a moron!**

3. "*Do you guys live on the ship*"?

Answer. **You are a fuckin' moron!**

4. "*How do I know which pictures mine*"?

Answer. **You are a fuckin' moron and should be shot in the face!**

There are a-number-of other such questions, but we will get to that later. So, for future reference, if you feel you have an overwhelming desire to ask a dumb question, don't be disappointed if the person you are addressing does not answer. They have far better things to do than talk to imbeciles.

It was about six o'clock and time for a recce on how this fine ship worked. I had a three-hour break, so dressed in my work-out-kit I had a mooch in and around the atrium, the shops, the gym and then the restaurant to try and establish what went on.

The focal point of a cruise ship in the nineties was the main restaurant. Each passenger was designated a time slot, either early or late, which was a necessity as 'The Sov' carried nearly three thousand passengers. Two sittings of breakfast, two sittings of lunch, two sittings of dinner, the now infamous *midnight buffet* and a plethora of other eating establishments that catered for the hungry masses. It was a fat person's dream, all looked after by busboys, waiters, maitre'ds, sommeliers and an army of KPs and chefs. Subsequently, it was responsible for anywhere between seventy to eighty per cent of the crew, and as a result of that, it is the biggest run mafia organisation at sea. Two sittings of breakfast are one shift, and a waiter has to do twenty shifts a week, meaning out of twenty-one possible shifts per cruise they get one-off. If they are not particularly good at their job or get a rotten review from a passenger, they also get to do the midnight buffet, so a typical day for them would generally consume about twenty-one hours of their day. *Yes!* Three hours sleep before they get to go through two breakfasts, two lunches, two dinners and all the cleaning and preparation that goes into keeping the restaurant spick and span. So, the next time you are on a cruise, and you think to yourself that the waiter always seems to be there, it is because they are. And the answer to the question, don't you ever sleep? Very little. In labour terms working in a restaurant on a cruise ship is in complete contravention of employment law. You are not expected to work to these

191

horrendous hours it is demanded of you, their way or the highway, so to speak. It is why you will never see an American working in such demanding circumstances because not only is it highly illegal, but they would not do it. We are talking about upwards of one hundred and twenty hours per week whilst at the same time being mentally and physically abused. The levels of bullying are off the scale, but because most of the team come from the third world, they put up with it. It can be quite lucrative in terms of the tips, but the systemic abuse of those that are not in management positions is something I found distasteful. They will argue that in order to maintain standards, they needed to keep people on their toes, but in my view, that is complete bollocks. How can it be right that a person in the restaurant can be expected to work these hours whilst at the same time maintain a perfect work ethic? That is why the question, *why are you not smiling*, drove me mad! I would make a point of giving an answer of something like, what do you do for a living? You're in construction, are you? Do you smile all fuckin day? No, you don't, so jog-on!!! There I said it, someone had to say it. You must smile through the pain which at times can be trying, so that it is one of the reasons that class 'A' recreational drugs are so prevalent on cruise ships. It is necessary. The mafia side of things kick in when they want/need/require a shift off. In my day it cost ninety dollars to have two sittings of whatever off, that you paid to the maitre'd, who got a kick back from the restaurant manager where most of the readies landed. So, if you wanted a twenty-station meaning you looked after two tables of eight and a table of four you had to pay a percentage of your tips for it. These were where the big bucks were earned because they were serving forty clients. More importantly American clients, and they are big tippers. If you look after them, they will look after you, it is the fundamental principle of how the mechanics of finance work in these environments, so you can only imagine the clamour to secure one of these roles. The waiter looked after the maitre'd, he looked after the section manager, they all greased the palms of the guy at the top. If a restaurant manager completed a yearlong contract without any breaks, he would comfortably earn north of a million dollars in that contract. Do the math.

I smelt an opportunity. Upstairs-downstairs is the perfect example of the two faces of employment at sea as you get to see the real characteristics of what a certain individual is going through. Upstairs is for the passengers, below decks is our time and where the real partying goes on. Once we have catered for their every whim, it is our time, and boy do casino staff know how to enjoy themselves. Because we worked mostly at night, we were segregated from the rest of the crew in our own little section called 'slime alley' and after every shift you would hear someone mutter the immortal words 'slime time'. This was a call to arms that was synonymous with the entire casino staff as one of the main reasons that you worked at sea was to get drunk. A maintenance of your alcohol levels was an essential ingredient in those days as many a time I spent recovering on a beach. My break finished I went to work safe in the knowledge that cocaine was a commodity in use by the crew and that made it easier to move. On to the next stage. We did Labadee which was more than pleasant as I got to spend it in a hammock with Elnima.

Fresh from a good sleep and an early night it was time for more analysis and research. I had breakfast in the windjammer watching 'The Sov' sail into SJ before I made myself double busy. The object of the exercise was to have a look at how the security detail worked and after two hours of observation I concluded, it was easy. I had a light lunch then we all caught the bus to the football pitch where we had organised a referee and got on with the game. To my surprise there were some proper footballers on display. There was Christian an Australian goalkeeper that had earned a living playing in goal, the British contingent of myself, Andy and Nick the photographer', the 'sweaty mafia', two Costa Rican's, a Jamaican and a couple of others that I can't remember where they came from. An eclectic mix of players that went on to form one of the best sides that ever sailed the seven seas. It was a strangely competitive game with no little given, and none taken. I was delighted as the standard was much better than I imagined. I went to see the hotel manager and gave him the good news. We had our first game on Saturday, and I explained to him it would be in his favour to come and have a look and see what he thinks. With a job well done, a pocket full of readies and a proper sort on me arm, it was time for Old San Juan.

Now that we had established who the footballers were and the long-term strategy of the team, we could finally relax in each other's company. Even though we were from different parts of our Island's there exists a knowing etiquette between players. It is a teamwork mentality that I carry to this day. I'll watch your back and you watch mine. So, with that in mind we went as a group to various bars, the Small World then Lazers. It was the start of something big, it was the start of the best time of my life.

The best cure for a San Juan hangover was Magen's Bay. So, after breakfast in Havensight it was off to the north side of the beach which was the furthest from the taxi drop meaning it was the quietest. It was and is one of my favourite places to visit in the world particularly with a beautiful young woman, so after cavorting in the water for a bit we decided to have lunch on the beach. Life was going swimmingly to coin a phrase, however that was about to take a drastic change. Elnima and I, were having a shower when the cabin door flew open.

"Get on the ground, get on the fucking ground now"!

Then in as deep a voice as is humanly possible, I replied, "That's going to be a little difficult".

The door to the toilet/shower room opens with a customs officer and a dog giving us the once over.

"What the fuck is going on here"?

"What do you think is going on, my girl and I were having a shower".

"Together"?

"It's not against the law is it"?

"No one likes a smart arse".

"No one likes a prick either!"

"What did you say? Get your asses out here"!

With that a female colleague of his interrupts, "Hi guys, we are just doing a routine check. Can you both put towels on and vacate the cabin please"?

This was a much softer approach that worked.

"But of course,"!

Suitably attired, we step into the corridor whilst the dog does its thing. Approximately two minutes later they all appear, "Sorry for disturbing you, have a nice day"!

I don't know why but I breathed a sigh of relief, my heart was beating like a jackhammer, and I had the sweats, Elnima says, "You got a guilty conscience"?

If only she knew. This spooked me as this was a turn of events I never saw coming,

"I have never seen that before".

"Seen what"?

"Seen them".

"Really"?

"First time".

"Sweet"!

Music to my ears. We went back to what we were doing and two full days at sea.

One of the best kept secrets about Miami is that it rains a lot. It has a tropical climate as it has never been recorded below sixty-three degrees Fahrenheit, but it is wet. On this day of all days, it was raining cats and dogs. Fucking pissing down it was. For all intents and purposes, I loved playing football in the rain but in this type of heat it was nauseating. The 'sweaty mafia,' Andy, Nick and I struggled at first but as we grew into the game the difference in ability was there for all to see. We were clearly head and shoulders above them and the score line of eleven nil was a fair reflection of proceedings. To say the hotel manager was delighted is an understatement so when he came and knocked at my door by way of an invite for dinner it was no surprise. Another factor was the quartermaster Abner was also a football nut and being of Costa Rican extraction enabled him to get a blow-by-blow analysis of each and every game. This of course did me a favour as I will explain later, he inadvertently helped me in my little business venture.

Work was going well, we won all five of our games, my girl and I were getting serious and by now I knew the mechanics and logistics of the ship. It was time to go and see the boys in Puerto Rico. At the next San Juan I slipped a note under the door at the Small World stating that I would be back at 3pm for a drink and something else.

Juan and the boys were waiting for me when I got there.

"Let's go somewhere else".

I demanded.

"Good idea".

I didn't want to be seen with such company at that time of the day as it would arouse suspicion, so we went deeper into SJ than the passengers and crew were told to go. Also, there was only ever Abner on in the afternoon and because of that I knew he wouldn't search me.

The boys and I get down to business!

"First and foremost, I don't want to meet a lot of people. I get the gear from you and deliver it the other end to nobody. How this works is I get the gear on in SJ and off in Miami. I book into the Marriott and put the sniff in the safe. I drop the key to the room and the combination to the safe to a girlfriend of mine that works at Hooters in Bayside. You simply get your courier to pick it up from her and Bob's your Uncle!"

"You've done this before David"!

"Once or twice"!

"How much can you carry"?

"We'll start off small so give me a kilo"!

Without anyone saying a word a bottle of tequila appears, "One other thing I want to make clear is that this is the end of our relationship. We don't see each other, we don't socialise, nothing. The last thing you want in these circumstances are people asking questions because they are too fucking nosey"!

"I like you David".

As far as I was concerned the meet was over.

"Go and get the gear boys"!

"We'll be back in five".

They came back with the yayo, I asked for a number to call from Miami and told them I will call at twelve in the afternoon.

"It's five grand your end"!

"We have it here"!

"That's not how I work"!

They both looked at me suspiciously.

"You pay me next week".

"Shall we bring the thing with the money".

"No. I'll pick it up from Gio sometime in the evening. This is not a weekly gig. The indicator when we go to work will be a note under the bar asking for a meet"!

I left and went back to the ship to hide the contraband and go see Elnima.

San Juan, St Thomas and two more sea days came and went before our first real test against a team on Saturday that were supposed to be as good, if not, better than us. As a team we were starting to develop. I stressed this to the HM, as he was getting excited because he could see the potential. He had not been to a game for a while but through various sources he found out that we were going to be tested this coming weekend, so it was no surprise to see him among a crowd of more than three hundred, which must have beaten the previous record by about two hundred and ninety-eight, such was the reputation of both teams. We had a full-strength side out, meaning we dominated the game. We eventually won two nil, with Nick the photographer grabbing both goals to go along with his mounting tally. Game finished I grab my bag and drop the gear off at the hotel, went back to the Seaman's Centre, called the boys in Puerto Rico and looked forward to a week on 'The Sov' and Elnima.

San Juan was sweet as I got the readies from Juan and told him to be ready in a couple of weeks. The boys passed on their regards and hoped they would see me soon. And that's how it was for a few more weeks. Played football, went to work, and done a couple more drops.

It all came down to the last game of the season. We won all our games; The SS Holiday won all of theirs. A potential battle of titanic proportions. Before the game I gave the best speech of my short managerial life. I reminded them that we were from all parts of the globe but, had managed to build a team based on organisation and spirit. We had come so far, (literally) and we were not going to let them (SS Holiday) spoil it. As I was giving my team talk, I hadn't noticed that 'Pancho' a Costa Rican with immense football ability was missing until I went through what each player's responsibilities were. He was one of if not our best player and I, no we, really needed him. I made an enquiry with his mate,

"Where is he"?

"He can't make it until half time boss"!

"OK Jimmy you'll take his place until he gets here and then you are coming off".

"Sweet".

The sizeable crowd were getting vociferous as we walked out. You could feel the atmosphere, it was palpable. Then we got the worst possible start. Tackles were flying in as you would expect but of all the things you don't need in a big game is going down to ten men. In a game of this magnitude, it was the last thing we needed, but as the Glaswegian red mist descended, Magoo decided to go flying in two footed to crunch their player in the (Niagara's). Fucking ice-cream, I can still hear the scream as he nigh on snapped in him half. To the dismay of the crowd Magoo was red carded. No Pancho and now no Magoo, two of our best players to sit alongside me in midfield was going to be an uphill battle, but not against the run of play we opened the scoring. I played in our centre forward who beat their keeper all ends up. One nil to 'The Sov'. A strike of immense quality. The heat and the fact we were a man down was proving difficult, but we got to half time still leading but no Pancho. About five minutes in to the second half, they scored. One all!

We were hanging in there, even going close on a couple of occasions when suddenly there were some rummaging' amongst the crowd. They all had their backs to the game and were shouting something in an urgent fashion. It was Pancho, running at a fair clip taking his clothes off, preparing to put his kit on. I motioned to the referee immediately and gave Jimmy the thumbs up, a firm handshake and a heart filled thank you as he walked off to be replaced by Pancho. With a real appreciative round of applause in his ears and Pancho walking on like he owned the place a sequence of events occurred that could be described as some of the best I have ever been lucky to be a part of.

We had a throw in which I received, with one touch I turned and gave it to Pancho. With his first touch he went round one then another and from fully thirty yards hit a screamer into the top corner, a strike of absolute quality. Cue mayhem.

The crowd went berserk as there was only a minute left. We saw the game out, were crowned champions and had a party the likes of which 'The Sov' had never seen. I remember getting to work a mess but because of adrenaline the alcohol was not registering. Throw in the fact I had a couple of bumps of Bolivian marching powder, and you get some idea of the state I was in. The Hotel Manager appeared with Abner full of the joys of spring and a promise that he would be buying the beer that night. Abner was smiling like a Cheshire cat. The whole casino was buzzing, it was a fantastic day to be alive.

I was sitting box a lot now. Due to people finishing contracts etc, the old guard were changing, and I wasn't far away from the end myself. Then out of the blue the big boss himself showed up mid-cruise wanting to speak with me. He asked me what I thought about RCCL, "May we have a frank and candid exchange of views"?

"Go right ahead".

"The contracts are too long. Nine months becomes a test of endurance after six, you are burnt out by that stage".

"What about the casino"?

"What about it"?

"What do you think about our policies and procedures"?

"They are ridiculous"!

"I thought you might say that. Elaborate"!

"How much can I elaborate"?

"Say what you like David, that's one of the reasons I came on board"!

"No come-line on dice, just a massive field".

"Go on".

"The odds offered are wrong and the constant changing of dealers who are deemed unlucky is beyond the realms of stupidity".

"I thought we had stopped doing that"!

"If I was a passenger, I would not play in your *pretend* casino".

This struck a nerve as he winced when I mentioned that. So, imagine my surprise when he said that he wanted me on the Majesty, the new ship that was launching in a couple of months.

"My number one question is this, why are players discouraged from taking full odds? They are in the houses favour for fucks sake! Why, do you change the stick if he calls three winners and lastly, why do you change the bones during a roll?

"You have raised a couple of interesting points. I like the odds-on dice changing because as a going concern we need to address that. How about you draught a new policy and procedure manual for me to have a look at with the prospective changes".

David knew the company was going global by expansion so therefore to go with their current protocols would have been disastrous.

"The other stuff I shall run by the managers"!

We had a couple of drinks, said our goodbyes and David promised to confirm the details of the trip to join the Majesty. I ran straight into the arms of Elnima. I didn't have the heart to tell her about the conversation I had just been involved in. My future with the company looked good, however that would mean doing it without her. I was excited but broken hearted at the same time. How the fuck was I going to explain this?

We still had about a month to go so I went to see Juan to explain that our little business deal was over. It was fun while it lasted but it was time for me to concentrate on my future in the casino business.

When I went to work that evening a funny thing happened, the manager asked me to keep an eye on proceedings as he needed to speak to the management team. A hand started to develop on dice and quite a big crowd were gathering when the stick starts giving me shifty eyes. There is another point made (or a winner by the shooter), when it became obvious that the stick is getting extremely uncomfortable.

"Do you need to go the toilet or something"?

"No".

"What's the matter with you"?

"I'm singing".

"Your what"?

"Like a canary".

I sit down as there was no Boxman and anyway I wanted to prove a point.

"Taking you off the stick is in no way going to change the nature of the game. Be professional and the game will look after itself"!

The crew were immediately lifted. The next person that went on break, told whomever else was on a break who then told someone else and so on. A little break from the pathetic protocol that existed brought a great deal more professionalism and at the same time got me noticed. It worked. I upset the applecart culminating in me getting called to a meeting.

"There is a rumour going around at the moment".

I was unaware of any rumours, so I protested, "I'm sorry".

"You left a dealer on the stick singing up a hand"!

"I beg your pardon".

I was praying he would persist. Fucking moron, he went on.

"Why did you leave him on"?

"I am not going to answer that question".

"Why not"?

"It is not company policy".

"I'm in charge, you do what I tell you to do"!

I just laughed at him. I genuinely hoped he was going to get aggressive as he was a complete prick!

"If I recall properly, you weren't there. In my eyes the game was being professionally dealt with no mistakes and more importantly the passengers were having a great time".

Got him. I had him. I had him from the very fucking beginning. What sort of casino manager believes in this policy, believe it or not at the time they all did, it was frightening. He stormed off with his tail firmly between his legs.

I only had a couple more cruises to go so the manager kept out of my way and I kept out of his, a mutual respect and appreciation of the other's abilities. I certainly didn't hold any grudges against him because given the same set of circumstances I may have done the same thing, but the game was changing, it was time to alter the system.

I was sat box all the time now, there was a fantastic casino crew on board, we were earning good money but at the back of my mind was Elnima. I tried to ignore the decision by getting stuck in to writing the new procedure manual, but my mind kept wandering. I couldn't focus! Eventually I started to think about what I was good at. I thought about penny-up-the-wall and how I grasped the concept of when violence was going to raise its ugly head. I thought about the dogs and how certain dogs would have solo trials so the trainer could determine why a dog was not performing as it should, and as a result of that trial, it would produce a much better result next time out. I thought about dealing an illegal poker game to men that could be considered a menace to society and how I managed those games seamlessly, all before I was sixteen. I thought about that recruitment day at Stringfellow's and how I was given a second chance. I thought about the training school, Charlie Chesters and how I eventually ended up on stick, on dice/craps. I thought about football and why I decided not to chase that dream.

And then it all made sense. I don't know whether it was divine intervention, pre-determination or a massive set of coincidences but I was born to do this. It was in my blood. It is what I do!!!

From the basis of that thought process I had to make a heart-breaking decision. I knew it now. I wasn't the same after that. We get to my last cruise, and I played the excited guy that had just experienced an unbelievable nine months. We partied all week, we laughed, cried, I said goodbye to friends, acquaintances and colleagues. It was a great week but at the same time it was fucking horrendous. My girlfriend and I held on to each other the entire week hardly saying a word. I had not experienced anything near this intensity in a relationship in such a short period of time. I was in deeply in love with her, but I was twenty-nine and in the prime of my life. I was selfish, I was wrong but, in my eyes, there was so much more to see and do. I was a first-class cunt who put his career first. Looking back, I could and should have handled things entirely differently and with the benefit of hindsight I would have, however it is a heavy price to pay for being a decision maker, and from the bottom of my heart I am sorry for ending it the way I did. Earlier in the book, I refer to falling in love. I said that it only happens once. *Not true!!!* I can say hand-on-heart, they were the best nine months of my life.

13

Sun, sea, sand and San Miguel. I was off to the land of the cheap. I had been home for a couple of days, but my head wasn't right, so I flew into Girona Airport, hired a car and went in search of some R&R along the beaches of the Costa Brava. Even though it was early March it was warm compared to England.

On my first port of call, I walked into a restaurant ordered a drink and asked for a menu. The first thing that struck me was no-one spoke English. There were no ex-pats, no football shirts and no drunken Herbert's like there is in the summer. It was bliss. The only problem being is they had no pictures on the menu and as my Spanish is very limited this was going to be of some concern. Fortunately, one of the chef's had an English girlfriend and on hearing of my predicament came to the rescue. I gave him free rein to make me something local, which I have to say was very tasty, washed down with a couple of lager-beers and got down to what I was here for.

What was I going to do with the rest of my life? What was I good at? What did I enjoy doing? And more importantly, what was available?

I was in my early thirties, fit-as-a-fiddle, with enough readies to have a year off. I wasn't ready to settle yet as I still had bundles of energy and I wasn't finished with the States. I wasn't going back to my previous life as believe you me, I am no villain.

I drank the last of the wine, asked for the bill and before I paid it, I had decided. I was orf! I wasn't going to hang about in the land of *sangria* as it would be hard work translating and all that, so I booked into a hotel, reserved a flight to New York via London for two days and fucked right off!

It was too quiet in Spain and as I am a council estate kid, I like noise and lots of it. I love the constant sound of kids playing, adults rucking and reggae music. I find it soothing. So, when I landed at JFK, I instructed the driver to take me to the heart of Manhattan.

14

Once again, I found myself at the Chelsea Hotel. It was seven o'clock, so I went for a stroll. Approximately four hundred yards west on West Street was an Irish bar with real Irishmen that sold shit Guinness. So, when they asked for ID, and I produced my Irish passport I was welcomed with open arms. The conversation very quickly turned to circumstances –

"You on holiday?"

"Yes and no!"

"What does that mean?"

"It means I'm on holiday for a couple of weeks then I'm going to Miami" –

"Have you got a green card?"

"No!"

"I won't ask. What do you do?"

"I'm a casino guy"

"You're a dealer?"

"Yes" –

"That's great. Me and the boys are off to Atlantic City on Friday if you fancy it?"

"Sounds good!"

"It'll be some craic!"

"I'll have some of that and while you're at it, pour us another Guinness please" –

"Coming right up" –

That was handy. Not only did I make some potential new friends. but I was going to play cards too.

I did the usual stuff one does in midweek NYC. Had an overpriced meal at a pre-show restaurant, went to a couple of clubs, twin towers, empire state, all the archetypal tourist stuff before we get to the weekend in Atlantic City.

It was one of my new friends' birthdays, so as a bonus they hired a limo for the return trip. It was luxurious, with champagne, cocaine and cigars from Havana. We checked in at Ceasar's and like all gamblers that haven't had a bet for a while, I headed straight for the poker room. I bought into a 2/5 Texas hold'em game for a thousand dollars, took my seat and made introductions. This was nineteen ninety-four and we were still a long way from the Moneymaker effect so, with that in mind I set about the table.

Ever since I was a child, I have had a profound love of cards. Patience/solitaire, three card brag, seven card stud and my all-time favourite, five card stud – one down, four up, stripped deck to sixes, aces count in a baby straight. There is a button, small blind, big blind with all players dealt one down – one up and the betting starts under-the-gun when all players have received two cards. There is a round of betting and then another street is dealt and so on. In my opinion, it is by far the best card game as you can play it blind drunk. It is engaging, fun and hilarious if you get the right table.

However, we are in the nineties and there are nowhere near the complexities or professionalism around there is today, so dare I say, it was relatively easy making money on a poker game.

A common myth I would like to dispel right here and now are there are a lot of poker professionals that consistently make money. *Not true!* It doesn't matter how good you are, there is still an element of luck, and you will suffer bad beats, no matter how many times you are ahead and in the right spots, it's the nature of the beast. The number one priority in poker is bank-roll management but unfortunately you must be ultra-disciplined and at the end of the day we are human beings dictated to by our emotions. Unfortunately for me I fall into that bracket of being a gambler, so if I am in the right spot, against a weaker player and I have a flush draw to the river, I will call, I cannot help it, it's in my nature. Other players wouldn't do what I do and that's what makes them better, but we are in two-thousand and twenty-two and every man and his dog know how to play Texas Hold'em, both tournament and cash.

There is so much prize money these days that I get the clamour to want to play the game, but there is no fun in it anymore unless you go to Ireland! I'll give you an example; There is a big tournament that runs between the UK and Eire of which I played in the two biggest. In Dublin, you couldn't get to the bar as it must have been five or six deep. In England where it was held at The Amex Stadium in Brighton there wasn't a sole at the bar, just lots of guys standing around with their sunglasses and earphones on.

In my very humble opinion, this is the wrong type of environment as the whole essence of playing live is the social interaction and aggravation. Having a few light ales loosens the tongue and heightens the emotions. A major bug bearer of mine is the wearing of sunglasses and being allowed to hide your entire face. Now, I am not for one minute suggesting that you can get reads, but letting players hide on a table is just wrong. The whole essence of playing live is to goad other players. *That's why I play live!!!* If you find the atmosphere of live-poker intimidating, then fuck-off and stick to your keyboards. I've even heard players say it's a gentleman's game and should be played accordingly. *No, it's not!!!* Rugby is a gentlemen's game! Pokers a game played by liars, spivs and shysters. That's the essence of the game! What do you think a bluff is!?! Look at that situation regarding, Will (like a boss) Kassouf in the World Series. He was in no way shape or form out of order, all he was trying to do was get information by verballing his opponent, who called him mean. *What?* Don't be so pathetic, man up, and grow some fucking balls. As long as you not holding-up the game, and there are only two of you left in the hand, you should be able to '*sledge*' your opponent. And my number one favourite in all of this, is the televised stuff. I'll say it, it must be said, poker is not a televisual sport, not in its current format it isn't. It is going the same way as snooker. In nineteen-eighty-one the World Championship of snooker was contested between Steve Davis and Jimmy White and attracted a television audience of roughly a third of the entire nation. Fast forward forty years and I doubt whether anyone you know is even interested in the sport anymore! Why? Because it is boring. Let me put it another way, it is the perfect cure for insomnia. The players are much more professional, clean-cut, therefore better but in my day, there were notorious for drinking and taking various substances. It made it watchable because the players were liable to get up to all sorts. In today's world of no emotion poker, quite frankly, I would rather stab meself in the face than sit and watch! It is about as much fun as piles!!!

I had about two and a half thousand in front of me when I got a sniff of the dice table. It is the most exciting gambling game in the world, but even better to play in the States, so I left the poker game immediately. Enroute to the craps pit one of the Irish boy's collars me.

"What you up to?"

"Gonna play some craps!"

"Where going to eat. Want to join us?"

"No thanks. I'll have some fun on the table!"

"Great, if I don't see you later, I'll see you tomorrow!"

"Sweet, enjoy your meal" –

I done me bollocks in about half an hour, but I was buzzing. I went to my room, picked up my unpacked bag, ordered a cab and took a hundred-dollar ride back to the Chelsea!

There is so much to see and do in New York City, but I couldn't stop thinking about the beach. The Big Apple is an absolute monster in terms of differing degrees of life, that will envelop you if you let it. I was ready, but not yet. I couldn't fight the desire and sheer craving for Miami. It ate at my soul. I tossed and turned all night thinking of what to do next. I had six nights left on my booking, but as soon as the alarm woke me at eight, I was up and ready in half an hour. I changed my reservation, checked out, got breakfast and made my way to La Guardia for an internal two-and-a-half-hour flight south to Miami.

15

It was strange getting in the cab and making our way south on the 95, as it felt more like home than Shepherds Bush. I was travelling light so; I asked the driver to drop me off at the News Café. I ate al-fresco, cleared my head, headed south along Ocean, located a realtor and went to view a one bed apartment on the corner of Third and Washington. With a deposit of a thousand bucks and six months' rent upfront there was no need for the usual rigmarole. I was in. It was still early doors, so I looked at the king size bed and took a snooze in preparation for the evening's festivities.

I jump in the shower and get ready to let South Beach have it. I head east toward Ocean and then north toward The Clevelander. I defy anyone to give me details of a better spot-on earth, than Ocean Drive, South Beach, Miami, in the early evening of a Saturday. It is paradise for singletons. There is so much good-looking fanny it is as if you are in a dream. I'm up three blocks chatting up two interested proper-lots, when who should pull up beside me but, Donnie and Gio. I know these two are brothers, but it is as if they are joined at the fucking hip, and what are the odds of them driving, and me walking past at the exact same time?

Donnie & Gio

The epitome of old-school mobsters. Built like brick-shithouses, they were a walking, talking catalogue of gangster chic. From New York to LA to Miami, it was as if these guys all have the same tailor. Both night and day they were immaculately dressed. They could be charming; they were courteous, but the swagger they carried was one of menace. A real throw back to when men-were-men! I had a great relationship with both as I kept a lid on it. It was one of mutual respect. I liked both and they couldn't give two fucks about me.

"Where the fuck are you going?"

No basic civilities, no it's been a while, just straight to the point. The way I liked it.

"I was going to have a light ale!"

208

"Get in the fucking car!"

Here we go!

"Have you eaten?"

"Not yet" –

Fifteen minutes later we are in one of the nicer food establishments in this part of the world. The table is furnished with not one, but two bottles of Dom Perignon, the waiter hands out the menu's and we get down to business.

"What are you up to?"

"Nothing as I just got here!"

"Are you going to ………."

"No chance. I'm probably going to look for some casino work on the boats" –

"Funny you should say that! We own one!"

"What, really?"

"We were only talking about you the other day" –

"Tell me more" –

"We just bought it David, but it's not our field of expertise"

"You want me to look after it for you?"

"Exactly!"

"You don't know what I can do?"

"We have worked with you before. You're good, professional" –

"When?"

"Two weeks"

"Sounds good"

I couldn't believe it, my own boat. Yes, it was a small operation, but if I get this right, it will lead on to other things. There were a proliferation of these boats attempting to satisfy the insatiable need to gamble by the inhabitants of Florida. In essence it created its own cottage industry and I happened to be in the right place at the right time.

"Do we have a deal, David?"

"Fucking right you do!"

Cue a loud raucous round of laughing. Suitably cheered up and not a little lagging, (it's the bubbles) we get on with the meal …….

"Do you play poker David?"

"Is the pope a catholic?"

"We play in a private game in Lauderdale. Texas Hold'em, five, ten, twenty, forty, obligatory straddle. Fucking good game. Fifty grand minimum buy-in. The first time we played was last week. I get into a hand in the first ten minutes. I'm under the gun with aces, so I make it fifteen hundred, the button calls. The flop comes down, ace, deuce – deuce so I lead out with five large. He shoves for fifty grand, and I snap him off. The turn and the river are bricks, so I table my hand of aces (full), looking at the hundred grand and this cocksucker turns over two little ducks. Fucking quads. The very next hand Gio has ace-king suited, gets involved with the same guy. It all goes in the middle pre-flop when both players turn over their hand. The English guy turns over eight-deuce off, so Gio looks and winks at me. The dealer dealt a rainbow brick board, followed by the same on the turn and then miracles of all miracles, dealt a deuce on the river. Motherfucker!!!"

"Did you say English guy?"

"Yeah, lucky motherfucker!"

"What did he look like?"

"Good looking kid!"

"How did you get in the game boys?"

"What?"

"Who invited you?"

They look at each other.

"Where's this going?"

"Because it sounds like you got turned over!"

"Explain!" –

"There is a remote possibility you could have lost against quads with aces full, but it is highly unlikely. I very much doubt you would have got called for fifteen hundred with deuces pre-flop. He may claim he was set-mining but then to hit quads and call fifty grand with eight-deuce off and hit on the river. Absolutely no chance, the odds of that happening are infinite. You can take it from me fellas, you got fucked!"

"Motherfucker!"

"So, I ask you again. How did you get in the game?"

"Some fucking broad!" –

"When? How?"

"I was in a club having a drink when she came over, we got talking then one thing led to another. Before I know it, I'm getting my knob polished then she gave me a number to call if I fancied a game. So, I call it!"

"And?"

"Some English guy answers, talks exactly like you. Tells me to come to this address in Lauderdale on Saturday. It was a real professional set-up!"

"You're telling me!"

"For fuck's sake Donnie, tell him"

"What was his name?"

"Donnie?"

"Tommy, I think he said his name was Tommy?"

"Do you mean Tom?"

"Yeah, that's the guy!"

16

Three and a half hours north on the 95 and we arrive in Port Canaveral. She wasn't pretty, she wasn't much of anything, but she was mine. One hundred and twenty feet long and about sixty feet wide, 'The Kissimee Star' would house gambling on two levels. She was old and out-dated but seaworthy. I was paid the ultimate compliment by the boys who entrusted me to run this operation. We embark to be met by people of varying degrees of responsibility, when I can only assume the captain asks for order.

"We'll make introductions as I give you the dime tour" –

This was a bit of me, I went about my business quietly, but assertively! After lunch, we were given the logistics, start times for cruises etc and informed we began cruising twice-a-day, Wednesday – Sunday, in two weeks. I made my way to the Cruise Director by way of an intro.

"I'm David"

"You the casino boss?"

"I am!"

"I've heard a lot about you!"

"All good I hope?"

"Absolutely. You ready for this David?"

"I've never been more ready in my life!"

"Follow me to my office"

Donnie, Gio and I enter ….

"Two floors of gaming, what's the plan?"

"Off the top of my head, we'll have two five-pound craps tables, ten blackjack, two roulette and a Caribbean Stud downstairs with roughly two hundred slots. Upstairs, one craps, three blackjack, one roulette and again a Caribbean Stud table. With about a hundred slots" –

"Three dice tables?"

"We'll need them at the weekend, and another thing. You need to move the cash desk!"

"What? Why? It's convenient where it is, you cash out straight into the lounge or get in line for when we dock" –

"A cash desk in a casino should be at the furthest point away from the front door. It's the same with selling bread and milk in a supermarket!" –

"Sorry, I don't understand?"

"More than ninety-five per cent of shoppers buy milk and bread in a supermarket, which is strategically placed at the furthest point away from the entrance, so the client must walk back through the shop and the packed shelves. The same applies to a casino. Having cashed out, a player will have readies in his hand as they walk back through the entire casino. We'll place a one-dollar game of roulette next to the cash desk and watch our hold go through the roof. It's a tried and tested formula!

He looked at me with a big smile on his face and if I didn't know any different, both Donnie and Gio had a glow of pride. Then the CD looks at the boys,

"You were right, he's our guy"

"Fucking right he is!"

We're back on the 95 heading south when I broach the question.

"How much?"

"Thousand a week!"

"What? how about fifteen hundred, plus two per cent of the win!"

Silence, then ….

"Slots and tables?"

"Yes!"

In stereo.

"Deal!"

17

The sound of the cars horn alerted me that the boys were outside. I get in the car and what can only be described as an air of hostility. We head north-west to the 95 and the hours' drive to Fort Lauderdale for a meet with the unsuspecting Tom. You could have cut the air with a knife, so I spoke slowly and surely.

"Before anything goes down, you have to let me get the readies!"

"What?"

"When we get there, I'll wait in the car for ten minutes whilst you get comfortable and then I'll knock on the door. I'll make basic introductions, produce my fifty large and then work out how they mugged you off!"

Stone cold silence. Not a dickie-bird! I pushed on.

"You have to create the impression that you have no idea what's gone on!"

They both turned around and gave me this look!

"Go through the normal meet and greet routine, then as you sit down, tell them you have another player coming, heightening Tom's expectations. They won't sus it's me and I can't wait to see their fucking faces!"

Again nothing!

"Boys please promise me you won't do anything I regret!"

We finally arrive and Donnie and Gio exit the car without so much as a fuck-off!

As the door opens, I'm peeking over the top of the back seat. There are two lovely young women at the door and the boys have smiles as wide as the Everglades. The girls move in for a hug and a kiss, with the chaps only too happy to oblige.

So far, so good!

As they enter the room, the retinue stand as one with warm handshakes and basic civilities.

The girls go to work. In their mid-twenties was one a blonde and the other a brunette. They worked the VIP area in clubs on the beach getting people who paid for tables upgrading them to buy even more expensive drinks. Extremely attractive, they were the epitome of how to flirt and mingle and create the impression they were more than interested in you, hereby getting you to believe you could fuck them, but the truth of the matter was very different. To them it was just a job. The blonde wore a black silk number, the brunette white, exposing just enough breast, midriff and thigh to drive a hot-blooded-male berserk. It worked the week before, but what they didn't know was we had a cunning plan.

After a couple of hands, the doorbell rings with little 'ol me barging his way into the action.

It was an elaborate house that overlooked the ocean. The shag-pile carpet enveloped your shoes, the furniture stank of expensive leather and the pictures on the walls doubled as a gallery, with local artists advertising and selling their wares. The drinks cabinet contained various whiskies, cognacs and wines, with ridiculously sized Cuban cigars and a mountain of Columbia's finest if you wanted to go down that route too.

It was a stunning setting!

As I enter the room the dynamic changed completely. It went from congenial and friendly, to awkward and uncomfortable. The so-called players, consisting of an archetypal South American, complete with ponytail and what looked like three typically flourishing Floridian businessmen, started clearing their throats, looking down at the table, and generally giving an air of not wanting to be there. As for Tom, he went a funny colour.

I got the scam in two seconds. On cue the girls approach the boys, sit on their lap and whisper sweet proposals in their ears. 'Anytime you fancy going next door, I'll suck your ….!" You get my drift. At the same time the waiter is reloading the dealer's water on a table, whilst switching the deck. The dealer picks the new set for seven players up and Tom gives the girls the signal the cards have been changed. I witnessed all this as I walked in the room. The players, the girls, dealer and Tom knew it too. I walk to the table and declare in as loud and assertive cockney voice I can muster; "Let's play cards boys!!!

The dealer glances nervously at Tom, who is looking for a shovel to dig himself out, whilst all-the-time the two boys are laughing their heads off safe in the knowledge, I had rumbled their little scam. (I don't get these things wrong)!

"Before you pitch the cards, do you mind shuffling again as I am a little old-fashioned like that!"

In an instant, he dropped his head, his bottom lip starting protruding and his hands started to shake.

I was UTG, so I straddled for a hundred dollars. The cards are dealt, UTG+1, MP and the cut-off fold, Tom raises to five hundred from the button, both blinds fold leaving me to act. I look down at six-three off and raise to three thousand. Tom instantly mucks. At this point it is worth mentioning that although Tom was a shyster of the highest order, he knew I was the much better card player, and on top of that he liked his face the way it was.

For the next half-an-hour, we played out the charade of playing a real game of hold 'em, when in reality it didn't matter what his holdings were, or how the betting went, I had to win until the boys got their one hundred and me, my two hundred large. It was an essential part of the experience because if Tom hadn't played his part, he was going swimming with the fishes.

"It's been a good evening; I think I'll call it a day!"

Cue stunned silence!

They clearly hadn't countered the fact that we were going to win so they were one hundred and fifty grand short. One of their group stands up …. "How short are you?"

"A lot"

"No problem, give me half-an-hour!"

Donnie and Gio grab the girls and bring them into the adjoining room, leaving me and Tom alone. "I, I…"

"Do yourself a favour and keep your fucking muggy faced mouth shut!"

"At least let me …."

"I've just told ya, keep schtum!"

I sat staring, enjoying watching him squirming in his seat!

"How do you know them?"

"None of your fucking business!"

"What's gonna happen next?"

"Who knows?" I shrug. "I think you're coming with us!"

His eye started twitching.

"You need to talk to them!"

"I don't need to do fuck-all!"

"But, but …."

"You know the rules!"

"I, I …."

"Turn it in, have some fucking dignity!"

He starts pleading for his life.

"For fucks sake Monz. Talk to 'em!"

"First and foremost, they are not my friends. I did some work for them that's all. Next, I'm going to look after a little gambling operation of which they own. That's my world, you know that!"

"But I, but I …."

The door opens. It's one of the players with our readies. I count it, knock on the door adjacent to the room and inform Donnie and Gio we are good to go. Donnie opens the door topless, with his belt undone and his flies open. "You count it?"

"Yeah, we're good!"

"Give us five" –

Even in moments of intense pressure, you'll find a man's brain in his dick. But to be fair, looking at the girls I didn't blame them! They came out ten minutes later with the girls resembling a date with a typhoon. Donnie tips the girls, then looks at Tom …. "Get up, you're coming with us!"

It was pointless protesting!

In the car, the talk very quickly turns to congratulations.

"Well done cock-er-ney!" In the worst attempt at a London accent I ever heard.

Half-an-hour later we pull into an industrial estate and enter an old dis-used warehouse. Gio points the shooter at me. "Get out the car!" So, I follow his lead.

"Something's not right!"

I forgot where I was.

"you're telling me. I get your readies back and you're pointing that at me!"

"Donnie, get that cocksucker out here!"

Tom is shaking uncontrollably now" –

"Take your clothes off" –

Donnie tries to hand me his gun. "Shoot that mutha!"

"Are you off your nut?"

I took the pragmatic approach and stood in front of Tom. "I'm a casino guy for fuck's sake. If you have a problem with a game whether it is craps, blackjack, roulette or poker, you get me to sort it, Thats what I do!"

"I'll shoot the pair of you" –

"Fuck you!"

"He done you for two hundred and us for a hundred large" –

"Did!"

"What's the difference?"

"I got it back!"

"So?"

"So, killing him ain't gonna solve anything!"

Donnie looks at Gio, Gio looks at Donnie. They both look at me! "Get in the car" –

I do as I am told. Then Gio produces some lighter fluid, pours it over Tom's clothes and throws a match on it. As tom's clothes go up in flames ….

"We better not see you again, because next time you won't be so lucky!"

The two boys put their side-arms away, get in the car and we three drive off into the three am Miami heat!

18

After a week of topping up my tan, I call Donnie regarding recruitment for the ship.

"Who's looking after the crew?"

"Bobby!

"Who's Bobby?"

"Our business partner!"

"I didn't realise" –

"He's the casino guy, he's from New York! We told him all about you!"

"OK" –

"Give him a call, he's expecting it" –

That threw a spanner in the works. I thought I was going to be in charge. I call him ….

"May I speak to Bobby please?"

"Speaking!"

"My names David Moynihan" –

"The English guy that thinks he's Irish!"

"Something like that!" –

"Can you come to New York David?"

"When?"

"Tonight" –

"I'll need to buy a ticket!"

"I don't need your life story. Call this number when you get here, and I'll get one of the boys to pick you up!"

"Perfect" –

At approximately ten pm I arrive at La Guardia. I call the number Bobby gave me.

"Where are you?"

"The airport"

"Which one?"

"La Guardia"

Bobby lifts his mouth away from the phone, "Carmine, go pick this kid up from the airport!"

"Sure thing Bob!" –

"He'll be thirty minutes!"

"Sweet!"

I put the phone down and go in search of a bar and a nice cold beer.

. . . .

From the Battery to Harlem, there is never a dull moment in the city that never sleeps. From the movie 'Once Upon a Time in America' to Alicia Keys performing the song 'New York' featuring Jay Z. There are nowhere near enough superlatives to describe the Big Apple!

Approximately thirty minutes later a car pulls up with two guys. Just as I thought, this guy ran an illegal game in New York backed up with some considerable official clout. These were proper mobsters. I started to think that I was in way over my head, but it would be good to have a look anyway. It couldn't do me any harm; I am just a small fish in a very big pond. As soon as I arrived Bobby made it more than clear that he liked me. He brought me into a back room and explained that the boys in the other room had their own fields of expertise.

"I have some bad news. I've just put the phone down with Donnie and Gio and informed them the boat is not going to happen. Our people in Florida didn't grease the right palms so the IRS have impounded the boat"

"OK, but why have you asked me to come up?"

"Donnie and Gio spoke very highly of you, said you was a smart kid!"

I never said anything.

"Anyway, I need someone to run my craps table for me here in New York!" –

"Are you offering me a job?"

"It's not difficult to work out who am I David"

"No"!

"Would you be OK with this"?

"What about the cozzers"?

"The what"?

"The police"!

"No problem"!

"How about I do one night and see how I go"?

"Perfect".

"When"?

220

"Friday at seven".

"I'll be here".

"Oh, by the way, it's only you on the game".

"No drama, see you Friday"!

What the fuck was I doing, what was I thinking of? This was proper big boy shit. I flew back to Miami to pack lightly as I was only working Friday and Saturday night. I would maintain the apartment as I had no worries where money was concerned so I went back to New York early Friday with a spring in my step.

This was always going to be the most difficult chapter to write as I have a profound love of New York! As we speak, I am getting excited just going over the positivity this city gives me. I hail a cab and find a cheap hotel; I get settled in and ordered lunch without any alcohol. I must be taking this seriously I thought as I was guessing you must be on point with these guys and turning up smelling of alcohol is not a good move. Soon as lunch was done, I made the call,

"Is Bobby there please"?

"Bobby who"?

"I'm sorry I don't know his second name".

"When you find out let me know, now fuck off"!

"Before you go, can you tell him it's David the casino guy".

"Hold the line".

It went dead for what seemed ages then, "It's Bobby, where are you"?

"6th and Delano".

"Wait there"!

The driver arrives, "You are not staying here are you".

"I am".

"Go pack".

Five minutes later, I am back in the car, and they put me up at a much nicer place where they have influence. The one thing that surprised me was I had absolutely no nerves. I was as calm as the Dead Sea but eagerly looking forward to seeing what type of operation I had let myself in for. I hadn't noticed the door entry the last time as it was open, but now that it was closed it had that movie feel to it. I knocked on a cast iron door then a guy pulls back a little slide and say's,

"What the fuck do you want"?

"I'm the new craps guy"!

"Who"?

Someone else appears at the little gap, takes one look at me and says, "Hey Bobby, it's the fucking English guy"!

After what seemed like ten minutes the door opens, and I am met by two of Bobby's goons both giving me the once over.

"Turn around, hands in the air".

I have never been frisked before. It was kind of weird but necessary given the setting. Bobby comes over with a big smile on his face.

"Let me show you the table".

As it comes into sight I was delighted because it was a bog-standard craps table that was going to prove tricky to operate by virtue of dealing the game by myself.

"That's going to be problematic"

"It is precisely why I got you"!

"Thanks for the vote of confidence".

"You are very welcome".

Within an hour the game was mobbed. I was stood where the Boxman sits as I ran the game myself, no stickman, no basemen, no box, nothing, just little ol' me. I controlled the dice; I paid all the prop/ hard way bets as well as all the base bets. It was fucking hard work but illuminating as I got to add an additional piece of kit to my developing armoury. As we finish up the night, I had some complimentary comments in my direction and then it dawned on me we hadn't discussed the readies. I had completely forgotten to get a rate, so it was a surprise when Bobby comes over,

"The table made four large of which you get twenty percent".

Eight hundred dollars for a night's work was more than reasonable to me, "You get a flat rate of three hundred if the table does money. Do we have a deal"?

"Absolutely"!

"See you tomorrow at seven"?

"I look forward to it"!

I'm having some of this. How the fuck could I say no? All I had to do was my job. Don't engage, speak when you are spoken to, and don't say anything stupid. I thought I can do that. It was surprisingly professional as the firm had been told to leave me alone.

When I got in on Saturday, he was waiting for me.

"Were you paying seven to six on the big six and eight last night"?

"Yes, I was"?

"Why"?

His whole face changed. Here we go, I am in massive trouble now!

"Anything less than seven to six is not on. I think we are better than that"!

"I like that David, but before you make any more adjustments come and OK them with me first".

"100%".

Then in a very menacing tone he gets one of his guys to order a new layout without a big six or eight on it.

"Anything else David"?

"No just that".

Wow, he had listened to me. And the reason being that he had obviously been in a similar situation himself, whereby some Herbert is telling you what to do when you have a far greater depth of knowledge. You do what you are told but it still hurts because if someone would just listen to you the game would be much more profitable in the long run.

We get to the end of the night, and I had made about five hundred dollars when again he calls me over.

"I have sent you over a little something".

I didn't have a clue what he was talking about, so I just nodded. I get a ride home. The light comes on and, in my bed, dressed in some scantily clad underwear is a blonde courtesy of the boss. I was being seduced but I knew this wouldn't last long. It felt to me that something else was going on and I became suspicious when I discovered they were following me. It is amazing how different the world is when you are clean and sober. It's as if you are in a parallel universe. So as soon as I made my tail, I knew it was time to go. So did Bobby, so we came to a deal.

"Deal the game for another month and I will look after you"!

"That's fair enough"!

"I'll call the tail off. If you feel different in a month, we'll talk then if not we'll shake hands and say our goodbyes"!

"You are too good to me Bobby"!

I got rid of the apartment in Miami and got stuck into New York. I scalped tickets for Knicks games at The Garden, I scalped tickets for the Yankees and the Giants too. I went to see a lot of stuff on Broadway and all the time Bobby paid my rent and sent me over something to ensure I didn't get lonely!

The job was going well. From the street corners of Shepherds Bush to the Upper East side of Manhattan, I had arrived. Everything that had gone before, brought me to this point. I was off dice and running the pit now. Bobby used to leave early such was his faith in me. There wasn't a bet on dice, blackjack or roulette that I didn't know before the dealer even cut it out. The dealers, suits and players knew that too. I became the pivotal point for the club. Earned me a lot of respect, and not a little attention from the ladies. I created relationships with the clients, which got me into all sorts of favourable positions, as well as VIP entry to clubs/bars/restaurants, tickets for all the big American sports and rooms to the best hotels that New York had to offer. However, one night I was very indiscreetly followed home. Once inside I became acutely aware that something wasn't right so as a habit of mine, I checked outside the windows only to turn around and find two of the boys standing right behind me. Not good! With an overtly menacing tone, one of them says

"Sit the fuck down"!

So, a seat I take.

"What the fuck is it with you"?

"Do what"?

They both looked flummoxed. Clearly my colloquialism had caught them off guard.

"English cocksucker, sit there while we take a look around".

"It's a one bed apartment, fill your boots".

They weren't suspicious, they were just doing their job trying to put the frighteners up me, but I couldn't give two fucks. So, after about two minutes I say, "You done"?

They didn't say anything, just looked at me, then walked out.

It was time for critical thinking. I was getting in deeper than I wanted. I had done my time. I had been in New York more than

224

six months, I had what can only be described as a blast, but I was getting too comfortable. So, after a nice *cuppa-tea* I fell into a deep contented sleep, safe in the knowledge that I would inform Bobby of my intentions first thing in the morning.

The loud bashing on the outside communal door woke me. They were back. I let them in.

"Get dressed, the boss wants to see you".

I was being summoned, fucking summoned. This was double not good. If anyone knows how this works, this is probably the most terrifying thing you will ever go through but as luck would have it, I wasn't being sent for. I walk into the club to be met by Bobby, "How long have you worked for me David"?

"Six months".

"You had a break yet".

"No"!

"Good, you're going to Bermuda".

"I am".

"You are. You and Little Bobby are going on a cruise".

This wasn't the end of it.

"I just need you to do this little thing for me".

Fucking knew it.

"You need to go and see this guy and tell him to come to New York".

"I don't normally do this sort of thing".

"You are not going to threaten him, you are passing on a message. Don't worry, you get to see Ruby".

"How the fuck did you know her name? In fact, how did you know she was me ex"?

With a knowing smile, "Little Bobby will be round yours tonight with the details. Enjoy your trip".

As soon as I got home, I rang Bermuda to let Ruby know I was coming.

"Alo, love".

"With that accent it can only be one person".

"Ow R ya"?

"Missing you, where are you"?

"New York. I'm coming over next week for three days".

"No fucking way".

"Coming over on a cruise".

"Oh, baby I really want to see you".

"Me too. It will be great to catch up".

"Any danger you could bring some yayo with you",

"100%, how much"?

"As much as you can carry"!

"Sweet, leave it to me".

"Thank you, baby, see you next week".

"I'm looking forward to it already".

I put the phone down and immediately got to work. I sorted half a kilo of sniff, had a shit/shower and shave in ten minutes and got dressed in some proper schmutter ready to attack Manhattan. Man, I felt good!

Getting sniff onto a cruise ship is not a particularly difficult thing to do, neither is getting it off to be fair, so armed with my contraband I met Little Tony at the Port of New York on point and ready to go. We set sail at five pm on Sunday, arriving in St. Georges at seven am Tuesday morning. I had arranged to meet Ruby in Hamilton at two pm on the Wednesday as the ship sailed around to the other side of the island on Tuesday evening, in my eyes a good strategy as the crew were nice and relaxed by then, meaning they took their eye off the ball if you know what I mean.

I fill a bag of soiled washing and at the bottom I put a plastic clear box which is normally used for holding washing powder but was now full of cocaine. Little Bob knocks on the door agitated so him and I are getting into it when suddenly, I realised that we had cleared immigration as customs didn't ask us a thing or for that matter check the bag.

In case we were being watched I made the meet with Ruby at a launderette at the back of Hamilton, as this gave my washing story some authenticity. I drop Bob off at the Robin Hood and walk in with my bag, and as I do so the loud beeps of a car horn alert me to the fact that she is there. An older woman with a name badge walks past, so I asked her to keep an eye on my bag whilst I went outside to say hello. I'd forgotten how good-looking Ruby was, (mixed race with natural blonde hair and green eyes) but that's another story. We had a quick kiss and cuddle, before I go and get the contraband. As I approach the machine,

"Sorry love, where's the bag"?

"On the machine"!

My heart started to beat a little faster. Suddenly, I became aware that Ruby was looking at me horrified. She had obviously worked out what had just occurred. She screamed 'NO'!

"It's empty, where's the contents"?

"In the machine".

"What do you mean"?

"I didn't think you would mind dear, but I loaded the machine with your washing and used the powder in the box"!

I must have stared at her for all of five minutes before bursting into a fit of nervous laughter. I was bent over with my head going around in circles looking in the machine at twenty grands worth of sniff spinning on my undercrackers.

"Have I done something wrong dear"?

"No love, it's my fault".

Talk about kill the buzz. We get the most expensive washing in the world done, safe in the knowledge that I would be sniffing me smalls for the next six months.

As much as we tried to enjoy each other, it wasn't the same. We had an afternoon at the beach but there was something in the air. "I have something to tell you"

"Go on!" –

"I have a little girl"

"No way, you'll be a great Mum"

"After we broke up, I met this English guy. He reminded me of you" –

"That's not fair"

"I was still in love with you!"

"You split up with me love!"

"Anyway, he went back to England a couple of months ago and now I can't contact him"

"Seriously?"

"He gave me dodgy numbers and addresses, so I haven't got a clue where he is"

She starts giving me those eyes.

"I must go love. I'm chaperoning a pal of mine from New York for a couple of days. A right character!"

She looked at me with that same intensity. I had nothing in me. I kissed her on the cheek, wished her all the best and made my way back to the ship.

Little Bobby was waiting for me ….

"Have you been to see that guy yet?"

In amongst all that happened, I had completely forgot about the message. With the address in my hand, I get a taxi at the port and instruct him to take me to said Herbert.

On approach to the apartment, I suddenly developed a set of nerves. I got butterflies, very strange. To be honest I was a little apprehensive as I had never done this sort of thing before. I rang the bell – nothing, So, I rang it again, this time there was the familiar sound of footsteps hitting a wooden-floor.

"Who is it?"

No fucking way, it can't be. I never replied.

As she opened the door, she lifted her considerable hair and stood there staring intensely, curiously. Waiting to see what I would do. I looked into her eyes which now had tears in them. I just ran at her, she jumped up and wrapped herself around me for all she was worth. We kissed passionately as if to make up for lost time. "Hi!"

"Hi!"

"How did you?"

"That's a very good question!" –

"I actually saw you in New York"

"Where?"

"In the park" –

"Why didn't you …."

"I couldn't, I froze!"

"How comes Bermuda?"

"Why not?"

"Good answer" –

"What are you doing here?"

"I took a cruise, I'm here for another day or so"

"Would you like to come in?"

"Yes, I most definitely would!"

The next two hours were the most intense I have ever spent with anyone in my life.

It was Olivia.

We eventually settled down for something to eat. She was sitting on my lap with her arm around my neck staring into my eyes. "I'm coming with you!"

"What about Bermuda?"

"I've got no ties; I have a little money!"

I put my arms around her and held her tight. "I'm done with New York?"

"What do you mean?"

"I'm in too deep with the firm so, now's the time to chip!"

"What are we going to do?"

We both laughed out loud at that!

"Are you sure?"

"About what?"

"Coming with me?"

"I'm not letting you go this time!"

"I've got some money. Word has it that California is going to open casinos in the not-too-distant future. Might be an idea to have a look at that!?!"

"I go where you go!"

"That's settled then!"

"Just like that?"

"Just like that!"

We held hands as I walked her onto the ship and signed her on as a guest. Little Bobby was in the main bar surrounded. "I see you found her!"

"How did you know?"

"The boss done some digging. He really likes you David, thinks you're a smart kid!"

"Thank you!"

"Don't thank me, I didn't do anything!"

The ship took two days to sail to New York. Olivia was waiting for me at the airport.

"I got to go and see Bobby!"

We got a taxi straight to East 72nd between Park and Madison.

We enter the club and Bobby was waiting for me. "Come in here"

"You happy?"

"Extremely!"

"I got someone already to replace you. Some guy called Peck".

"Fucking Pecky!"

"Do you know him?"

"I met him once, but I've known him all my fucking life!"

"Is he alright?"

"Good as gold!"

"Before you go, I want you to think about something"

"What's that?"

"What you going to do now?"

"We're going to load the motor and head west I think"

"Good, because I have some people in California that would like to meet you!"

"Really?"

"Yes really. There will be new casinos opening, so they're going to need good people. Just like you" –

"That's very kind!"

"All I'm saying is think about it. You've got my number. If you need anything call me. OK son!"

"Thank you, Bobby!"

I had shed a brief light on New York, and it was time to go. We get back to my apartment, load the car, lock the front door and put the keys through the letterbox. I look up and down the road, peer into the car and Olivia, take a deep breath and bid farewell to New York!

Printed in Great Britain
by Amazon